BEGINNING AZURE® DEVOPS

T0312803

BEGINNING

Azure® DevOps

Published by John Wiley & Sons, Inc., Hoboken, New Jersey.
Published simultaneously in Canada and the United Kingdom.

ISBN: 978-1-394-16588-9
ISBN: 978-1-394-16589-6 (ebk.)
ISBN: 978-1-394-16590-2 (ebk.)

For general information on our other products and services or for technical support, please contact our Customer Care Department within the United States at (800) 762-2974, outside the United States at (317) 572-3993 or fax (317) 572-4002.

If you believe you've found a mistake in this book, please bring it to our attention by emailing our reader support team at wileysupport@wiley.com with the subject line "Possible Book Errata Submission."

Wiley also publishes its books in a variety of electronic formats. Some content that appears in print may not be available in electronic formats. For more information about Wiley products, visit our web site at www.wiley.com.

Library of Congress Control Number: 2022947336

Cover image: © ArtemisDiana/Adobe Stock Photos
Cover design: Wiley

SKY10044250_031423

ABOUT THE AUTHOR

ADORA NWODO is a multi-award winning software engineer currently works at Microsoft, where she builds mixed reality on the cloud. She is also the vice president of the Nigerian chapter for VRAR Association. Her work there involves creating more awareness for virtual and augmented reality technologies.

Apart from building and advocating for mixed-reality technologies, Adora is a digital creator and the founder of AdoraHack, a platform focused on connecting tech talents to learning, networking, and job opportunities. She has courses online that teach people about infrastructure automation; she has also published content on software engineering, productivity, and career growth.

Adora is the author of the popular book *Cloud Engineering for Beginners*. This book is currently helping a lot of people start their career as cloud engineers.

Adora spends a lot of her time on Twitter and LinkedIn sharing about her experience as a woman in tech. She is extremely passionate about the developer community and is driving inclusion for women in technology. She co-organizes community events for unStack Africa, contributes to open source, and speaks at technology conferences worldwide.

ABOUT THE TECHNICAL EDITOR

VINCE AVERELLO has been a professional geek for nearly 40 years. During those often funny, sometimes frightening, but always interesting years, he worked for about a dozen organizations lending his expertise to a variety of projects. Every one of them has been a learning experience, so now he knows a little bit about a lot of things ranging from the Internet to garment trucking. Vince lives in lovely midtown Bayonne, New Jersey, with his loving wife.

ACKNOWLEDGMENTS

MY DEEPEST AND MOST heartfelt gratitude goes to God for his blessings in my life and career. Without His guidance and support, I would not be where I am today. His unwavering love and grace have been a constant source of strength and inspiration for me.

I am thankful for the opportunity to work with the amazing team at Wiley on this project. From the very start, it was clear that everyone at Wiley was dedicated to making *Beginning Azure® DevOps* the best it could be. Their professionalism and attention to detail were evident throughout the different phases of the project. They provided insightful feedback and suggestions, which helped to improve the overall quality of the book. Working with the team at Wiley has been an honor and a privilege, and I am grateful for the opportunity to have learned from such talented and experienced professionals.

I appreciate their hard work and dedication, and I know that this book would not have been possible without them. I am looking forward to the opportunity to work with them in the future.

I am truly grateful to have such an amazing support system in my family and friends. Their unwavering support and understanding during the time I spent writing this book has been invaluable. Their encouragement and belief in me has been a constant source of motivation and inspiration throughout the writing process. It was not always easy balancing the demands of writing a book with my personal life, but their support made it possible for me to accomplish this task. Their belief in me has been a driving force, and I couldn't have done it without them. I am forever grateful for the love and support they have shown me, and I know that I can always count on them to be there for me. Thank you.

Finally, I would like to extend my thanks to the readers of this book. I also hope that this book will be a valuable reference resource whenever you need a fresh perspective or a reminder of the key concepts of Azure DevOps. I believe that the information and insights presented in this book will be of great value to you as you continue to develop your skills and advance in your career.

CONTENTS

INTRODUCTION

AS ORGANIZATIONS STRIVE FOR GREATER AGILITY AND EFFICIENCY in their software development and deployment processes, DevOps has grown in significance for software engineering teams. DevOps aims to automate the software delivery process from development to production by bringing together the teams responsible for development and operations. With this strategy, teams can deliver high-quality software to customers quickly and effectively while lowering the likelihood of mistakes and downtime. The advantages of DevOps have contributed to its quick rise in popularity in recent years as businesses look to boost productivity and boost customer satisfaction in order to remain competitive in today's fast-paced business environment.

Azure DevOps is a collection of tools and services offered by Microsoft to aid software development teams in the planning, collaboration, development, testing, and deployment of applications. It includes different tools that work together to provide a complete solution, such as Azure Boards for agile planning and tracking, Azure Repos for source code management and reviews, Azure Test Plans for testing, Azure Artifacts for managing and sharing packages, and Azure Pipelines for continuous integration and deployment. These tools can also be integrated with other Azure services to offer an end-to-end solution. It is designed to cater to the diverse needs of different teams and organizations, making it a widely used choice for software development teams.

Beginning Azure® DevOps starts with an overview of the concept of DevOps and then also covers an overview of Azure DevOps before diving into the various Azure DevOps services. By the end of this book, you will have a solid understanding of how to use Azure DevOps to improve your software development life cycle and will be equipped with the knowledge and skills to implement it in your own organization. You will also learn a few tips that can help you start and grow your DevOps career using Azure DevOps tools.

WHO THIS BOOK IS FOR

This book is intended for a wide range of readers, including those without any prior experience in DevOps who want to build a career in it, as well as early to mid-career software engineers, platform engineers, site reliability engineers, and other DevOps professionals looking to improve their skills. Additionally, solution architects and product/project managers who want to use DevOps techniques and Azure DevOps to manage their software development process will find it useful. The book covers the concepts and tools of DevOps and how to use Azure DevOps throughout the software development cycle. It is suitable for readers of all levels, from beginners to those with some experience, and will provide them with the knowledge and skills needed to excel in their DevOps career and deliver high-quality software.

CHAPTER OUTLINE

Chapter 1, "Introduction to DevOps," provides an overview of DevOps including its definition, history, the DevOps life cycle, benefits, and the current state of DevOps in the industry. It also covers the basics of DevOps, including its advantages and how it can be implemented to improve the software development process.

Chapter 2, "Introduction to Azure DevOps," provides an overview of Azure DevOps, its features, benefits, and services such as Azure Boards, Azure Repos, Azure Pipelines, Azure Test Plans, and Azure Artifacts. It highlights the benefits of using Azure DevOps for improved collaboration and faster software delivery and also covers the difference between Azure DevOps Services and Azure DevOps Server.

Chapter 3, "Managing an Azure DevOps Project with Azure Boards," explains what Azure DevOps organizations are and how to plan and create them. It also explains the concepts of Azure DevOps projects, including different types of projects and how to create them. It covers Azure Boards concepts such as work items, backlogs, boards, sprints, queries, and plans. The chapter also demonstrates how to integrate Azure Boards with GitHub.

Chapter 4, "Version Control with Azure Repos," covers the topic of version control and its benefits, as well as Git, a popular version control system. It explains how to create and import Git repositories on Azure DevOps and covers the concept of pull requests and how to use them. It also explains how to use Git tags.

Chapter 5, "Automating Code Builds with Azure Pipelines," provides an overview of CI/CD and how Azure Pipelines can be used in this process. It covers the features of Azure Pipelines and how to define and set up pipelines. The chapter also describes the components of Azure Pipelines and explains the concepts of agents and agent pools. It covers the different types of agents that can be used and the use of Azure Pipelines Build Scripts including YAML and how to write a build script.

Chapter 6, "Running Automated Tests with Azure Pipelines," provides an overview of software testing, including its history and importance in the software development process. It covers different types of software tests, such as unit tests, integration tests, smoke tests, regression tests, and end-to-end tests. The chapter also explains the steps for running software tests and how to set up testing in Azure Pipelines, helping readers understand the importance of software testing and how to effectively test their software using Azure Pipelines.

Chapter 7, "Creating and Hosting Source Code Packages with Azure Artifacts," provides an overview of artifact repositories and introduces Azure Artifacts as a tool for securely storing and managing artifacts during software development. It covers Azure Artifact feeds, including the different types of scopes available and how to create them. The chapter also describes Azure Artifact feed views and upstream sources and how to set them up. It also includes information on how to publish and download artifacts in Azure Pipelines.

Chapter 8, "Automating Code Deployments with Azure Pipelines," covers release pipelines and how they work in Azure. It describes the deployment model using Azure Release Pipelines and shows how to create a release pipeline, create a release, and use multistage pipelines. The chapter also explains what multistage pipelines are and how to create them in Azure Release Pipelines.

Chapter 9, "Application Testing with Azure Test Plans," provides an overview of the process of using Azure Test Plans for testing and managing the quality of software applications.

Chapter 10, "Infrastructure Automation with Azure Pipelines," provides an overview on how to automate the provisioning and management of your application's infrastructure using tools like Azure Resource Manager templates and Azure Bicep and the benefits of using infrastructure as code. It also covers how to use Azure Bicep in Azure Pipelines, including setting up the tool, creating templates, and deploying them using the pipeline, with an emphasis on pipeline authentication.

Chapter 11, "Exercise: Practice Using Azure DevOps Tools," introduces a sample project with different exercises that will enable the reader to practice the various Azure DevOps Tools and Services you have learned.

Chapter 12, "Starting a Career in Azure DevOps," provides an overview of how to start a career in Azure DevOps. It includes tips on how to find your first job as an Azure DevOps engineer, as well as the importance of finding a community to support your professional development. The chapter aims to provide guidance on the skills and qualifications needed to succeed in this field.

Chapter 13, "Conclusion," summarizes all you have learned in this book.

SUPPLEMENTAL MATERIALS

Additional content is available to all readers of this book at `github.com/AdoraNwodo/ SampleLibraryApp`. This includes a sample project that can be used as a hands-on learning tool to help readers gain practical experience with the Azure DevOps tools discussed in the book. This sample project can be used to help readers understand the concepts and techniques covered in the book and to help them gain the skills and confidence needed to apply these tools in real-world scenarios.

TO GET THE MOST OUT OF THIS BOOK

One major prerequisite for the book is that you have an Azure account so that you can follow through with all the steps illustrated in the different chapters. The process of creating an Azure account can be completed in a few simple steps. Visit the Azure website at `azure.com`, click the Try Azure for Free button, and follow the steps.

1

Introduction to DevOps

"It is through improving our ability to deliver software that organizations can deliver features faster, pivot when needed, respond to compliance and security changes, and take advantage of fast feedback to attract new customers and delight existing ones."

—*Nicole Forsgren, PhD*

What You Will Learn in This Chapter

➤ Definition and Overview of DevOps

➤ History of DevOps

➤ The DevOps Life Cycle

➤ The Benefits of DevOps

➤ The Current State of DevOps

➤ Summary

How do we build secure, resilient, and rapidly evolving systems at scale? This was the question that led to the birth of DevOps. Prior to DevOps, this was an important problem that organizations were facing. As time passed, software engineering evolved, and more innovative software has been built to provide solutions in interesting business sectors. This software is currently transforming and accelerating different kinds of organizations.

DEFINITION AND OVERVIEW OF DevOps

DevOps is a culture or a set of practices bridging the gap between two formerly siloed units, software developers (Dev) and IT operations staff (Ops), throughout the entire product development life cycle. The adoption of the DevOps culture, tools, and applications has empowered teams with the ability to build and securely scale their software development practices, engage customers to get feedback more efficiently, and ship software that helps organizations meet their business goals faster.

HISTORY OF DevOps

To appreciate where DevOps is today, we should learn what existed before it. The DevOps trend was born in 2007. Prior to that, software developers wrote their code and worked differently from the other IT professionals who tested and deployed the code. This meant that there was a huge disconnect in software development and deployment practices.

One of the major factors for this was that software developers and IT professionals had different goals within an organization. The software developers only wanted to write code for software, and the IT/Ops professionals deployed the code when it was time. This made the product feature release timeline really long; a software development team would work on a feature for months before handing it over to the IT/Ops team for deployment. The IT/Ops team would also take some time to deploy the large feature that was introduced to the application. This created room for software bugs, slow deployments, and unstable applications. Over time, releasing software of poor standards would affect the experience of any customer using the application.

Prior to DevOps, the waterfall methodology was largely used. This methodology illustrates software development processes in a sequential manner. This means each process must be completed before the next process starts. Figure 1.1 illustrates the waterfall methodology.

During this time, requirements were gathered and planning was done before any system architecture, design, or coding commenced. Once the software design was validated, programmers would start writing the code required to build that software. After software development was completed, software testing commenced, and deployment of the large application followed. Maintenance happens when the application is now live in production, and that is done in its own silo.

With this model, no version of the application gets deployed until late in the cycle, which means months of working without seeing tangible results. If requirements also change halfway through the project, the entire plan is destabilized, and the team might have to end the project and start again. In the early 2000s, as software engineering evolved and quick innovation became an organizational advantage, organizations started adopting the agile methodology for building software because it was iterative and more flexible for long-term innovative projects.

The agile methodology is an iterative way to build software applications. This model involves a continuous loop of planning, implementation, testing, and feedback in short cycles. With the agile methodology, organizations could now deliver value quickly to their customers. However, as time went on and the agile methodology became the standard for project management and software development, innovation was still moving fast, and the desire to automate processes and iterate faster came to the limelight. This was how DevOps came to exist.

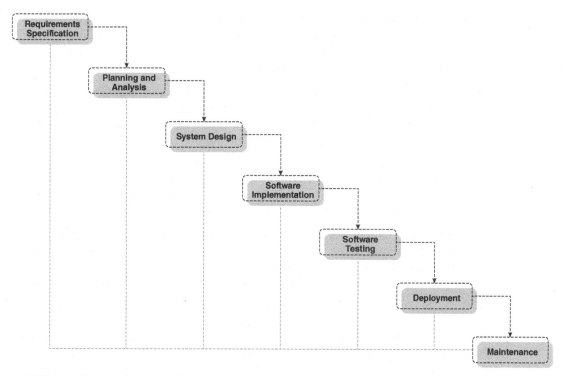

FIGURE 1.1: The waterfall methodology

THE DevOps LIFE CYCLE

With the DevOps life cycle, software development and IT/Ops teams are no longer siloed. The different steps integrate well with one another into stages for a broader and more cohesive engineering team. The stages are continuous, and the output of a stage is usually the input of the next stage. The stages are as follows:

➤ **Planning:** The planning phase involves teams identifying business requirements and then itemizing and strategizing for the different features of the application currently being built. This is an important stage in the management of the project. Here, the product teams also create a product roadmap and continuously track the progress of this task so that they can incrementally deliver and maximize value across the team.

➤ **Development:** During development, the teams work on different tasks created in the planning stage. This work involves writing the source code for the software feature. At this stage, different software developers are able to work on the same codebase simultaneously because of the integration of some DevOps tools that make this possible.

➤ **Continuous integration:** This stage commences when the software developers writing code integrate their own changes to the existing repository or codebase. This integration involves testing the code, merging the code to the larger repository, and creating build artifacts or executables that would be used during deployment.

➤ **Deployment:** In this stage, the output from the build step is deployed to different production environments across multiple geographic locations. Apart from source code deployment, application infrastructure can also be deployed in this step. This infrastructure is a foundational piece and the environment that the source code would run on.

For this deployment phase to be effective and secure, software development teams set up approvals and access policies for these production environments. This is important to control the deployments moving to production and anticipate the results of different deployments. This way, teams can automate code deployments with ease and confidence.

➤ **Monitoring and operating:** At this stage, a new version of software has been released to production and is currently in use by customers. The software development teams can now monitor user behavior, application performance, and other metrics. This monitoring helps teams improve the application so that they can always provide software with high availability to their customers.

With monitoring, software development teams can spot performance bottlenecks in real time and come up with solutions. If there is an error in the application, team members debug and troubleshoot until they can mitigate or resolve the problem.

➤ **Feedback:** User feedback is how teams improve on software. This involves communicating with customers to learn about their experiences using the software application. The output of the feedback process can be feature requests or application improvements. This output is usually the input for the planning phase of the next DevOps life cycle iteration (Figure 1.2).

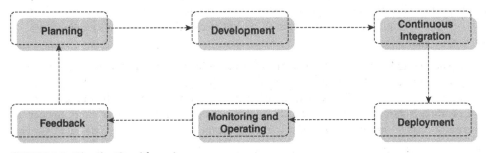

FIGURE 1.2: The DevOps life cycle

THE BENEFIT OF DevOps

The main goal of the DevOps culture is automation. The ability to automate different stages in the product development life cycle that were initially manual has the following benefits:

➤ **Speed:** As more tech companies come into the limelight, speed has become an important factor in innovating and keeping customers satisfied. DevOps makes speed possible. Teams can now build and release stable software in a timely manner due to automation.

➤ **Shorter release cycles:** DevOps teams implement the agile methodology. The agile methodology is an iterative software development methodology that allows teams to update software in bits, learn from that experience, and improve in the next software update iteration. Because of this, teams are not waiting to build out the entire application for as long as 18 months. Features can be iteratively worked on during short cycles called *sprints*; these cycles make code releases and debugging easier.

➤ **Collaboration:** DevOps fosters collaboration within teams. This culture eliminates the siloed approach to software development that once existed and makes it possible for team members with different skill sets (e.g., software developers, product managers, QA testers, site reliability engineers, etc.) to work cohesively together toward the launch of a product or feature.

➤ **Learning:** When software is released, monitoring starts. Here, teams are able to learn about the performance of their application and correct their mistakes to build better and faster software that their customers would enjoy. The DevOps model makes learning possible in the monitoring and feedback phase. Teams can learn from data obtained from logs, metrics, and traces. Teams can also take feedback from customers and learn from that experience.

➤ **Better quality products:** In multiple stages of the DevOps life cycle, DevOps tools trigger and run automated tests. The presence of testing reduces the number of bugs that get to production environments when the code is deployed.

➤ **Accountability:** In the planning phase in the DevOps life cycle, team members simplify processes, enumerate different tasks for product development, and assign all the created tasks to different people to work on. The culture of accountability is built because of this process. With this model, everyone knows what they should work on and their task is building quality software and deploying their changes on time.

➤ **Easier rollbacks:** Because code is released in bits, rollbacks can be done quickly if the need arises. It is a lot faster to roll back or redeploy smaller changes than it is to do the same for large changes to the codebase.

When applications have outages due to bugs, a new deployment, or a configuration change, a resilient DevOps culture where rollbacks can happen in a series of reasonable steps could be why outages don't impact many users and why organizations lose less money.

➤ **Security:** DevOps tools can integrate security audits into the product release life cycle to make sure that organizations are releasing high-quality and secure applications to their users. Integrating security into the building, releasing, and other continuous processes in DevOps is a practice called DevSecOps, which has also become popular in the application security sector.

THE CURRENT STATE OF DevOps

With the click of a button, the existence of cloud computing has made DevOps tools more accessible to organizations. Software development teams can build and test their code on virtual machines that exist on the cloud. Over the years, roles like cloud engineering, DevOps engineering, and site reliability engineering have sprung up to help organizations do cloud computing and DevOps better.

DevOps requires collaboration between the different stakeholders in the organization: software development, operations, and management. This collaboration makes building and releasing resilient software effortless. In globally distributed organizations where different team members exist in different parts of the world, DevOps and cloud computing are a powerful combination for digital transformation.

Cloud computing empowers teams all around the world to collaborate without manually sending files back and forth to team members. With the cloud, software development team members can seamlessly contribute to code in a shared repository, store build artifacts in an artifact repository, and store observability data (logs, metrics, and traces). This fosters collaboration, accessibility, and productivity.

Releasing quality software in DevOps would not be possible if multiple automated tests aren't run in different stages of the DevOps life cycle. The cloud also contributes to this by allowing teams to create virtual test environments for their application, taking away the pain of provisioning servers for testing and prototyping. This also contributes to the speed of software delivery.

Cloud computing makes the adoption of DevOps simpler today by accelerating each step of the software development life cycle. Different DevOps tools are software-as-a-service (SaaS) platforms that can be integrated with your organization's software development toolkit to improve quality and drive productivity.

DEFINITIONS

Cloud: A collection of servers and applications running on those servers that can be accessed through an Internet connection.

Cloud computing: The delivery of different computing services on the cloud.

Cloud engineering: The application of software engineering concepts in cloud computing. This involves planning, analyzing, implementing, deploying, maintaining, and securing applications that run on the cloud.

DevOps engineering: The implementation of DevOps practices in software development teams.

DevSecOps: The integration of security into every stage of the DevOps process.

Site reliability engineering: A set of practices that merges software engineering with application monitoring to make sure that deployed applications always maintain high availability.

Software as a service (SaaS): A cloud service model where the cloud provider runs and manages the application together with its infrastructure. Here, a lot is abstracted from the customer, who cares only about what they use.

SUMMARY

DevOps is a culture or a set of practices that bridge the gap between two formerly siloed units, software developers (Dev) and IT operations staff (Ops), throughout the entire product development life cycle.

Prior to the birth of DevOps, software developers wrote their code and worked differently from the other IT professionals who tested and deployed the code. This meant that there was a huge disconnect in software development and deployment practices.

The stages in the DevOps life cycle include planning, development, continuous integration, deployment, monitoring and operating, and feedback.

DevOps has multiple benefits including speed, shorter release cycles, collaboration, learning, better quality products, accountability, easier rollbacks, and security.

Cloud computing makes the adoption of DevOps simpler today by accelerating each step of the software development life cycle.

Chapter 2 introduces Azure DevOps. It explains Azure DevOps and distinguishes Azure DevOps from the Azure DevOps Server. It also describes the different Azure DevOps services and the part of the DevOps life cycle in which each service can be used.

2

Introduction to Azure DevOps

This chapter introduces Azure DevOps and the different services that Azure DevOps offers. Chapter 2 will also introduce you to Azure Monitor and DevTest Labs.

What You Will Learn in This Chapter

- ➤ What Is Azure DevOps?
- ➤ Azure DevOps Services vs. Azure DevOps Server
  - ➤ Differences Between Azure DevOps Services and Azure DevOps Server
  - ➤ Similarities Between Azure DevOps Services and Azure DevOps Server
- ➤ Azure DevOps Features
- ➤ Benefits of Azure DevOps
- ➤ Azure Monitor
- ➤ Azure DevTest Labs
- ➤ Summary

WHAT IS AZURE DevOps?

Microsoft Azure DevOps provides an end-to-end DevOps toolchain for developing and deploying software. It also integrates with most leading tools on the market and is advantageous for orchestrating a DevOps toolchain.

Azure DevOps provides services for software development teams to plan work, collaborate on code implementation, and build and deploy software products. Azure DevOps supports a collaborative culture and methodologies that bring together software developers, project managers, and contributors to develop software. It permits companies to make and enhance products quicker than orthodox software development approaches.

With Azure DevOps, there are various integrated components that you can access via your web browser or integrated development environment (IDE). Depending on your project and team's requirements, you may need to use some or all of the components, including Azure Boards, Azure Repos, Azure Pipelines, Azure Test Plans, and Azure Artifacts.

You can use Azure DevOps either on the cloud as a software-as-a-service platform utilizing Azure DevOps Services or as an on-premise tool with the Azure DevOps Server.

AZURE DevOps SERVICES VS. AZURE DevOps SERVER

Azure DevOps Services and Azure DevOps Server offer the same DevOps features. However, there are some differences to note, which we cover in this section.

➤ **Azure DevOps Services:** You can access the software-as-a-service offering for Azure DevOps through the Internet. This web-based service has a service-level agreement of at least 99.9 percent uptime, making it reliable. Azure DevOps services are also globally distributed.

➤ **Azure DevOps Server:** Azure DevOps Server's backing foundation is a customizable SQL server backend. If your organization embraces this version, you can access the on-premise offering over your internal network. This option is crucial for organizations that want all their data only on their own networks for business reasons.

Differences Between Azure DevOps Services and Azure DevOps Server

The differences between these two Azure DevOps offerings can be grouped into the following:

➤ Scoping

➤ Authentication

➤ Users and group

➤ User access management

➤ Data protection

Scoping

In Azure DevOps Services, scoping happens by *organizations* and *projects*. Organizations in Azure DevOps Services have URLs, and this is where everyone's collaboration journey starts. These organizations contain their group of projects. Each project can be developed and supported by the different teams in the organization, and team members need to operate in the project environment only.

With Azure DevOps Server, scoping happens by deployments, project collections, and projects. In straightforward terms, a deployment is a server. Project collections are containers that exist in deployments. These containers are for security, administration, and physical database boundaries.

They're also used to group related projects. Finally, projects encapsulate the different parts of individual software projects, including source code, work items, and more.

Authentication

Azure Active Directory is an identity and access management service.

In Azure DevOps Services, authentication happens over the Internet. Authentication happens with your Microsoft account credentials or Azure Active Directory credentials, depending on your organization's setup. You can also set up Azure Active Directory to require various features such as multifactor authentication, IP address restrictions, and more.

With Azure DevOps Server, authentication happens on an intranet server. You authenticate with Windows Authentication and your Active Directory domain credentials. This process is transparent.

Users and Group

Imagine a tech company that conducts multiple types of business for other organizations (business-to-business) and end users (business-to-consumers). In this organization, there could be different projects for different teams. For example, say there is the team building the SDKs and APIs (let's call them Alpha), the team building a customer-facing application (let's call them Diamond), and the team building and maintaining the company's website (let's call them Gamma).

In Azure DevOps Services, you can use an authentication method to give access to a collection of users. Use user groups to represent different teams in an organization. Using the scenario described, you can create Azure Active Directory User Groups for Alpha, Diamond, and Gamma. Teammates can join the user groups they belong to, and access to projects and resources for everyone is managed at the user group level. You can add these Azure Active Directory user groups to Azure DevOps Services groups.

In Azure DevOps Server, each deployment implements the user access methodology. Users can join Active Directory groups, and administrators can add these Active Directory groups to the different Azure DevOps groups. These user group memberships are consistent. So, when user access gets updated in Active Directory, it shows in the permissions the user has in that organization.

User Access Management

Beyond authentication, authorization exists to enforce that users have access to resources. This process happens by assigning roles and access levels to users. For example, a user with an Admin role will have permission to do more than a user with a Contributor role.

In Azure DevOps Services, each user has an access level, and they revalidate anytime they sign in. These users interact with resources only at the level specified, and that interaction happens on the Azure cloud.

In Azure DevOps Server, users have access levels, but everything happens from the primary system. Once the access level is specified, in addition to authentication, authorization occurs on the intranet server.

Data Protection

In Azure DevOps Services, all your data, including projects, source codes, and plans, exist on Azure. Projects in Azure DevOps Services are safe and secure.

In Azure DevOps Server, all your data exists on the on-premise servers your organization uses, and administrators control everything.

Similarities Between Azure DevOps Services and Azure DevOps Server

Although the cloud and on-premise offerings for Azure DevOps have some differences, they share some similarities as well.

Features

The cloud and on-premise offerings for Azure DevOps use the same components for code builds and releases, source code control, tasks management, test plans, and artifact administration.

Analytics and Reporting

Azure DevOps Services and Azure DevOps Server offer numerous tools that give you perspicuity into the activity and improvement of your software projects. Some of those tools include the following:

➤   Dashboards and lightweight charts exist in both the cloud and on-premises platforms. These tools aid in data visualization for various projects.

➤   Power BI is an interactive tool for visualizing data created by Microsoft, concentrated on business intelligence. Power BI integration helps teams to get analytics data into Power BI reports. With this, you will be able to analyze and visualize data from Power BI.

➤   OData support makes it easy for teams to instantly query the analytics service through the browser. Your product team can use the query result JSON as they want. You can generate queries that span many projects or your entire organization.

Process Customization

Both tools use the inheritance process model to customize their work-tracking experience. These customizations can happen instantly on the user interface or programmatically by calling the REST API endpoints.

Added Benefits On Azure DevOps Services

Although both Azure DevOps Services and Azure DevOps Server provide the same components and have some similitudes when compared with Azure DevOps Server, Azure DevOps Services offers some more benefits.

➤   **Simplified server management:** Azure eliminates the stress of handling the servers so your team can focus on other productivity drivers.

➤ **Access to the latest features:** When new features get released, Azure DevOps Services users access them before anyone else.

➤ **Improved connectivity with remote sites:** Since Azure regions are international, connectivity is better for remote teams using the SaaS application versus the on-premise infrastructure.

➤ **No upgrades:** Organizations running on-premise continuous integration / continuous deployment tooling deal with stressful upgrades. By migrating to a SaaS model, you worry less about fixing and upgrading the toolchain.

➤ **Expenses:** There is a transition from capital costs to operational costs. Capital costs consist of servers and the resources needed to handle all the infrastructure. Operational costs consist of subscription expenses for the cloud features you use. It can be difficult for organizations to spend a lot of money on capital costs, so operational costs introduce flexibility in expenses.

AZURE DevOps FEATURES

The following are the Azure DevOps features:

➤ **Azure Boards:** Software development teams can use the interactive and configurable tools in Azure Boards for managing their software projects. It delivers various features, including support for agile and scrum, customizable dashboards, and reporting. As your business grows, you can scale these tools.

➤ **Azure Repos:** Azure Repos is a collection of version control and source code management tools in the Azure DevOps toolset. Version control tools are applications that help you track changes you make in your code in real time. As you update your code, you tell the version control tool to take a snapshot of your files. The version control tool saves that snapshot, and you can retrieve it later when needed.

➤ **Azure Pipelines:** Azure Pipelines instantly builds and tests code to make them available to others. It combines CI and CD to test, build, and deploy your code to any target or destination.

➤ **Azure Test Plans:** Azure Test Plans is a test management platform with all the abilities required for different testing styles and gathering feedback from stakeholders. Some testing styles include planned manual testing, user acceptance testing, and exploratory testing.

➤ **Azure Artifacts:** Azure Artifacts allows software developers to share their code effectively and handle all their packaged code from one place. With Azure Artifacts, developers can publish packages to their feeds and share them within the same team, across multiple product teams or organizations, and even publicly.

➤ **Visual Studio Marketplace:** You can download extensions for Azure DevOps from the Visual Studio Marketplace. These extensions are created by Microsoft, in collaboration with the tech community. They are add-ons that customize and advance your team's venture with Azure DevOps. They can expand different parts of the DevOps toolchain, from managing work items to code integration and testing, pipeline builds and software releases, and team synergy.

BENEFITS OF AZURE DevOps

The following are the benefits of Azure DevOps:

➤ **Flexibility:** You don't have to use the entire Azure DevOps suite. It is attainable to adopt each of the services independently and merge them with your existing toolchain and process.

➤ **Platform agnostic:** Azure DevOps works with various operating systems (Linux, macOS, and Windows) and programming languages.

➤ **Cloud agnostic:** Azure DevOps supports continuous delivery to other cloud providers.

AZURE MONITOR

Monitoring is a crucial part of the DevOps process. Azure Monitor is not part of the Azure DevOps toolchain. However, it is recommended to incorporate monitoring because it helps you fully utilize the availability and performance of your applications and services.

Azure Monitor aids in maximizing your applications' availability and performance. It provides a complete solution for gathering and interpreting data from your application. This data helps you comprehend how your applications perform in production, and you can proactively recognize problems that need resolving.

Here's what you can do with Azure Monitor:

➤ Detect and analyze issues across applications and dependencies

➤ Correlate infrastructure problems with insights from the VMs and containers

➤ Create visualizations for logs and other kinds of telemetry

OBSERVABILITY ON AZURE

Metrics, logs, and traces are the three pillars of observability. These are the types of data that monitoring tools gather and investigate to provide adequate observability of a software application. To conduct observability, collect data from numerous pillars and aggregate that data across the entire set of monitored resources. Because Azure Monitor keeps data from various sources, the data can be linked and investigated using the same tools.

Azure Application Insights is a tool that observes availability, performance, and use for web applications. Azure Pipelines integrates with Azure Application Insights to continuously monitor your DevOps release pipeline throughout the software development lifecycle.

Monitoring is essential in the continuous delivery process. With continuous monitoring, release pipelines can include monitoring data from Application Insights and other Azure resources. When the release pipeline notices an Application Insights alert, the pipeline can roll back the deployment until the problem gets mitigated. If all checks pass in the pipeline, deployments can proceed instantly from test environments all the way to production, without needing manual intervention.

AZURE DevTest LABS

DevTest Labs is the place to practice using various tools on Azure. With DevTest Labs, software developers, testers, and other product team members can do the following:

➤ Build sandbox environments for Windows and Linux training. It is also possible to create test resource groups for exploring Azure using reusable ARM templates and artifacts.

➤ Create development or testing environments from CI/CD tools, IDEs, or automated release pipelines.

Exploring DevTest Labs is a good way to practice CI/CD in your journey to learning how Azure DevOps works.

SUMMARY

Azure DevOps provides an end-to-end DevOps toolchain for developing and deploying software.

Azure DevOps has two offerings. It can be used either on the cloud as a software-as-a-service platform using Azure DevOps Services or as an on-premise tool using Azure DevOps Server.

Azure DevOps features include Azure Boards, Azure Repos, Azure Pipelines, Azure Test Plans, and Azure Artifacts.

Continuous monitoring is an essential part of DevOps, and Azure Application Insights is a tool to integrate with the Azure DevOps toolchain for application observability purposes.

Chapter 3 is a deep dive into Azure Boards. There, you will learn more about Azure DevOps organizations and Azure DevOps projects. You will also be introduced to concepts such as backlogs, boards, plans, sprints, and work items.

3

Managing an Azure DevOps Project with Azure Boards

This chapter introduces Azure Boards and all its different features. You will learn more about Azure DevOps organizations and Azure DevOps projects. You will also be introduced to concepts such as backlogs, boards, plans, sprints, and work items.

What You Will Learn in This Chapter:

➤ Azure DevOps Organizations

➤ Planning Your Organization

➤ Creating an Azure DevOps Organization

➤ Azure DevOps Projects

➤ Types of Projects

➤ Creating an Azure DevOps Project

➤ Understanding Project Processes

➤ Concepts in Azure Boards

➤ Work Items

➤ Backlogs

➤ Boards

➤ Sprints

➤ Queries

➤ Plans

➤ Integrating Azure Boards with GitHub

    ➤ GitHub and Azure Boards Connection

    ➤ GitHub and Azure Boards Verification

➤ Summary

AZURE DevOps ORGANIZATIONS

An Azure DevOps organization is a tool for organizing and joining related projects. An Azure DevOps organization can be company-wide, or it can be for specific business units in your company. How you structure your organization depends on your use case.

Azure DevOps organizations give you access to the Azure DevOps toolchain, where you can perform the following:

➤ Schedule and track your tasks and issues with Azure Boards

➤ Work with software developers to build applications with source control management tools like Azure Repos

➤ Set up continuous integration and deployment with Azure Pipelines

➤ Create, organize, and share packages with Azure Artifacts

➤ Test applications end to end using Azure Test Plans

When creating Azure DevOps organizations, you should begin with one. As you grow, you can always add more Azure DevOps organizations. This approach is specifically valuable when your company has multiple teams that need to work on projects in isolation. These different Azure DevOps organizations can have varying security and structural models.

PLANNING YOUR ORGANIZATION

Having your Azure DevOps organization follow a similar structure as your actual organization is recommended. For example, imagine a large technology company that works on multiple customer products, software development kits (SDKs), and developer tools. They might have an artificial intelligence unit, a web development tools unit, and a cloud computing unit. Each business unit in the organization might function as its own organization, building multiple products with a vice president, engineering managers, software engineers, product managers, product designers, and more. In cases like this, each organization can have its own Azure DevOps organization, and each organization houses projects for a particular business unit.

Figures 3.1 and 3.2 illustrate this real-life organization and how they would be represented in Azure DevOps.

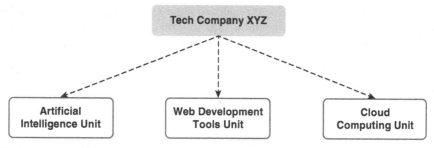

FIGURE 3.1: Business units within a tech company

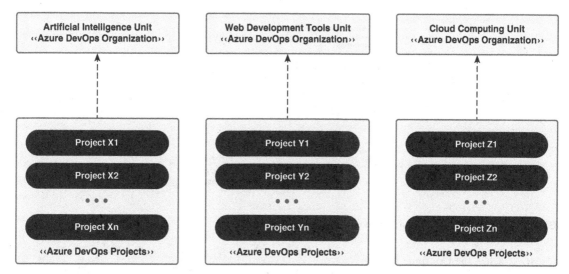

FIGURE 3.2: Business units represented as Azure DevOps organizations

CREATING AN AZURE DevOps ORGANIZATION

This section covers the steps required to manually create an Azure DevOps organization:

1. Navigate to the Azure DevOps website (dev.azure.com).

2. Log in with your Microsoft account credentials and select New Organization in the left sidebar, as shown in Figure 3.3.

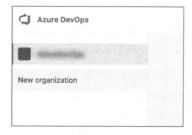

FIGURE 3.3: Creating a new Azure DevOps organization

3. In the pop-up window, name your organization and set the region where you'd like your projects to be hosted. The name of the organization in Figure 3.4 is AdoraDevOps, and the region is set to Central US.

FIGURE 3.4: Naming the organization and specifying project location

4. Click the Continue button.

On successful creation of the organization, Azure DevOps routes you to a page where you can create projects in your new organization. In the next section, you will learn about Azure DevOps projects and create a project within the organization you just created.

AZURE DevOps PROJECTS

A project is a store for data in Azure DevOps. Each organization can have many projects. Projects can contain the following:

➤ Boards and backlogs for project planning using the agile or scrum methodology

➤ Code build and release pipelines for continuous integration and deployment

➤ Code repositories for version control and management of source code

➤ Repositories for built and sharable artifacts

➤ Continuous test plans for the entire project life cycle

In the "Planning Your Organization" section, you saw how Tech Company XYZ splits each business unit into Azure DevOps organizations: Artificial Intelligence, Web Development Tools, and Cloud Computing. Tech Company XYZ's Artificial Intelligence unit has three projects within its organization.

➤ The **face recognition** project, which focuses on different SDKs and products for smart cross-platform face recognition.

➤ The **virtual assistant** project, which focuses on different SDKs and products for building and integrating virtual assistants across multiple devices.

➤ The **chatbots** project, which focuses on different SDKs and products for building and integrating AI-powered chatbots across multiple applications.

As you can see, these projects focus on different things. However, they all exist under the Artificial Intelligence Azure DevOps organization, which is connected to a single Azure Active Directory tenant. This means that team members working on any of these projects all have access to that tenant (Figure 3.5).

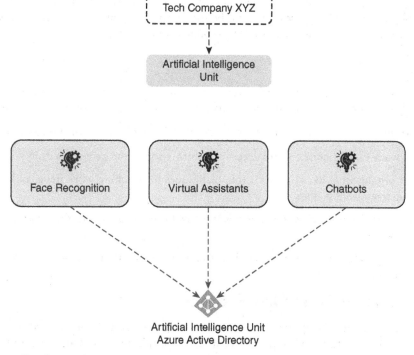

FIGURE 3.5: Azure DevOps projects

Types of Projects

In an organization, you can have a single project or multiple projects. In the example from the previous section, the Artificial Intelligence organization had three projects. This organization can also have one project with all the project items for the three subprojects compressed into one.

However, if more streamlined security between your projects and the teams working on each project task is a requirement for you, breaking down the projects is a recommended approach for creating that structure.

Single Project

A single project places all work at one level across the organization. In a single project, teams can share source repositories, build definitions, release definitions, reports, and package sources. You may have a large product or service managed by multiple teams. These teams are closely interdependent throughout the product life cycle. You create a project and divide your work using team and area paths. This setting allows your teams to see each other's work, thus aligning the organization. Your team uses the same taxonomy to track work items, making communication and alignment easier.

Having a single project is good for transparency, but it has its drawbacks. It's hard to find what you're looking for with multiple searches and boards. Depending on the product architecture, this issue may spread to other areas such as releases, builds, and repositories.

Many Projects

Having multiple projects shifts the managerial burden and gives the team more autonomy to manage projects as they see fit. It also provides access to asset and security controls within projects.

You may use multiple projects if your organization satisfies one or more of these requirements:

➤ You want to restrict or control access to information in the projects within your organization.

➤ Your organization likes to use custom techniques for tracking work items and tasks for its distinctive business units.

➤ Your organization wants to support respective business units with their own managed policies.

➤ Your organization may want to add custom tests or extensions before making changes to a project you're working on.

Creating an Azure DevOps Project

After creating the Azure DevOps organization, the Create A Project To Get Started page appears on the screen. To create a project using this form, specify a project name and visibility and then click Create Project (Figure 3.6).

After creating a project, you will see a dashboard with all the possible actions you can perform in the project. Azure DevOps projects are the starting point for everything you do. Figure 3.7 shows what the project dashboard looks like.

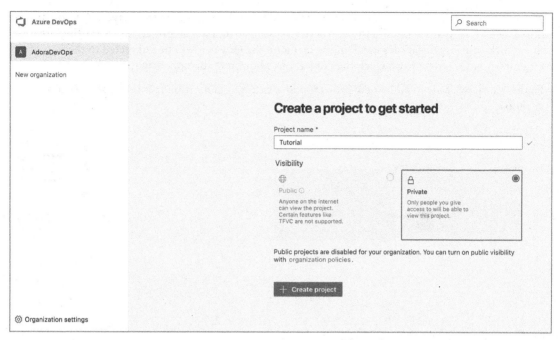

FIGURE 3.6: Form to create your first Azure DevOps project

FIGURE 3.7: Azure DevOps project dashboard

There is another way to create a new project. You can do this separately from creating an organization as well. There are many situations where you want to add a new project to an existing organization. Click your organization's name in the menu on the left. You will be redirected to the Organization Overview page. Click the New Project button in the upper-right corner.

Figure 3.8 shows how to add a new project to an existing organization from the organization dashboard.

FIGURE 3.8: Button for adding a new project to an organization

Clicking the New Project button displays a Create New Project form (Figure 3.9).

You can follow the steps to create your second project and many more projects if you like.

Understanding Project Processes

When your team initiates an Azure DevOps project, the team has to determine which process and templates to use. Processes and templates define the basic details of the work item tracking system used by Azure Boards. Azure DevOps supports the following processes:

➤ **Basic:** This is the most straightforward process that teams can choose. Track your work using epics, issues, and tasks. You can use this model when creating a new default project, as shown in Figure 3.10.

➤ **Agile:** Choose Agile if your team uses an agile planning process. You can track different work items, such as features, user stories, and tasks. Agile also uses a kanban board to track user stories and bugs. You can also manage them on the task board. You can use this model when you select the Agile process type as you create your project (Figure 3.11).

➤ **Scrum:** If your team uses the Scrum methodology, you choose the Scrum process. You can generate product backlog items (PBIs), tasks, bugs, and other work items for your team by leveraging the scrum process. You can also use kanban boards to track artifacts or break down PBIs and errors into tasks on task boards. Figure 3.12 illustrates the scrum process.

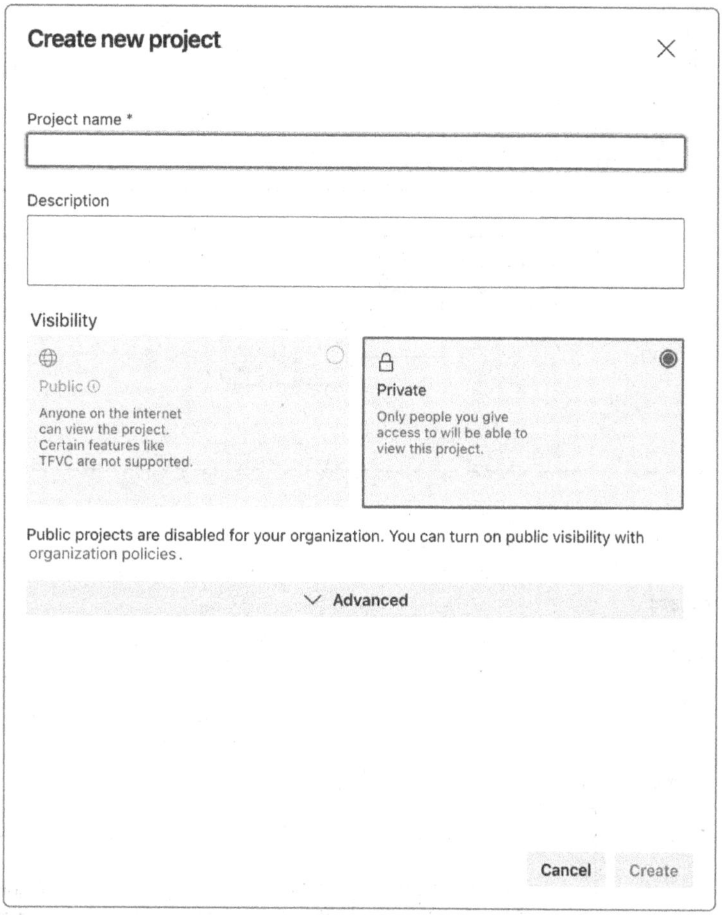

Create new project ✕

Project name *

Description

Visibility

⊕ ○   🔒 ⦿
Public ⓘ   Private

Anyone on the internet can view the project. Certain features like TFVC are not supported.   Only people you give access to will be able to view this project.

Public projects are disabled for your organization. You can turn on public visibility with organization policies.

∨ Advanced

Cancel   Create

FIGURE 3.9: Form for adding a new project to an organization

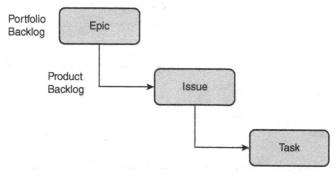

FIGURE 3.10: Basic process

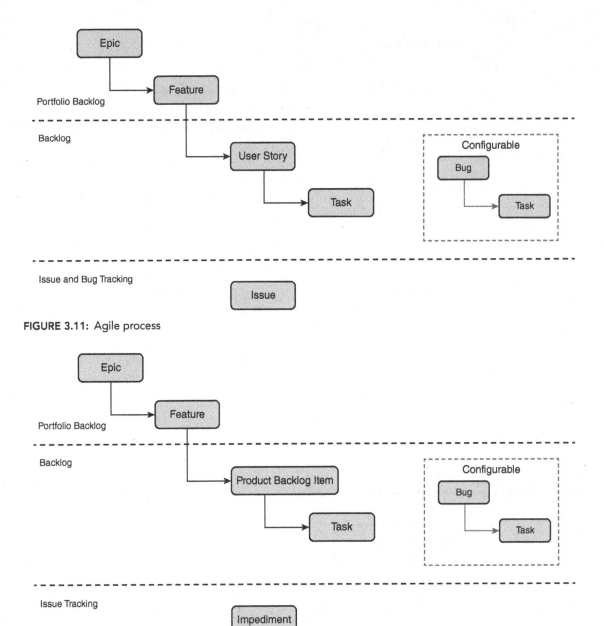

FIGURE 3.11: Agile process

FIGURE 3.12: Scrum process

➤ **CMMI:** The Capability Maturity Model Integration (CMMI) process is more appropriate when the team follows a more formal project methodology that requires a process improvement framework and a record of supportable decisions. This process model helps track requirements and change requests, risks, and assessments (Figure 3.13).

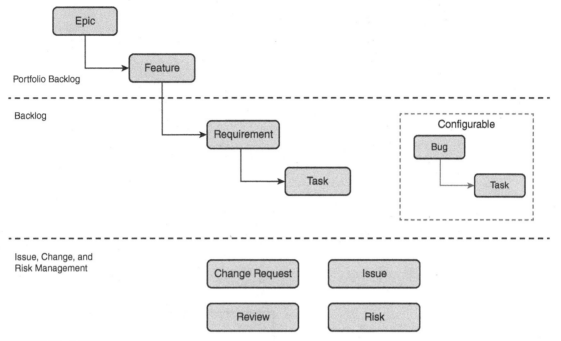

FIGURE 3.13: CMMI process

To choose a process for your Azure DevOps project, click the Advanced button on the form for creating a new project. The work items process drop-down menu has four processes to choose from. Throughout this book, you will be learning different concepts using the Basic process (Figure 3.14).

CONCEPTS IN AZURE BOARDS

Azure Boards give software development teams interactive and custom tools to oversee their product tasks. These tools include work items, backlogs, boards, plans, sprints, and queries. This section will cover the concepts in Azure Boards.

Work Items

Teams use work items to measure all the work done as a team. You can track features and requirements, code defects or bugs, and anything else. The available work items are based on the process selected when creating the project.

Work items in the Basic process have three states: To Do, Doing, and Done. As development goes on, the team members can edit the work items accordingly so that everyone has a holistic picture of the work related to the project.

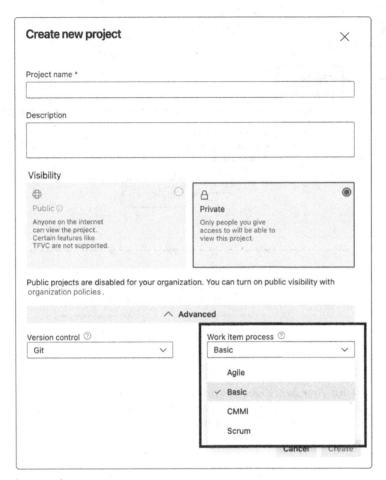

FIGURE 3.14: Choosing a project process

Creating a Work Item

This section describes the steps required to create a work item:

1. Go to your organization's dashboard and click the project for which you want to create a work item.

2. Click Boards ➪ Work Items to visit the work items listing page (Figure 3.15).

3. You should see a list of all your work items at this stage. Click the New Work Item link in the top menu. Here, you can see the different work items that can be created depending on the project process type selected during creation. As mentioned, we are using the Basic process, so we can create epics, issues, or tasks (Figure 3.16).

4. We will create a new task. To do this, click Task in the list of work items, and you will see a page similar to the one in Figure 3.17.

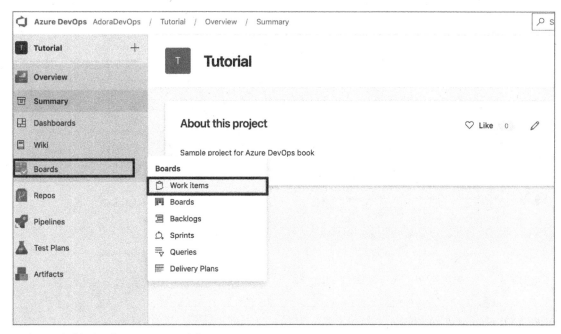

FIGURE 3.15: Navigating to your work items

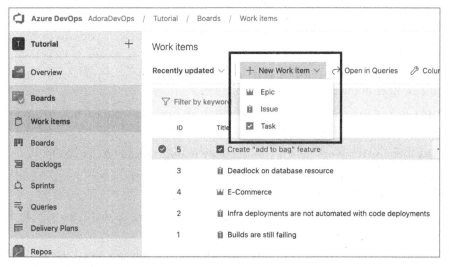

FIGURE 3.16: Work item types

FIGURE 3.17: New work item types

Now, enter the details for the task. The following are the fields and their meanings so that it is easy for you to know what to type:

➤ **Title:** Here, you can write the name of the task. (For example, create add-to-bag functionality for guest users.)

➤ **Assigned:** Here, you can assign work items to specific people on your team. This person must be a member of the project.

➤ **Add tag:** You can also add tags to this work item. You can use these tags to group related work items and find them later.

➤ **State:** Because this work item is new, the state is automatically set to To Do.

➤ **Iteration:** Here, you can define which sprint to add to this task. Setting the iteration can also happen later in the backlog.

➤ **Description:** Here, you can add more details about the task so that other people on your team have full context on the details of the work item.

➤ **Discussion:** Here, team members can post additional comments about the work item. You can have conversations here about tasks, pull requests, bugs, or any other thing relating to the work item.

➤ **Priority:** Here, you can set a number to indicate the priority of the work item.

➤ **Activity:** You can also classify this item. For this project, your work item can be classified as a deployment, design, development, documentation, requirements, or testing activity.

➤ **Development:** Here, you can link the item to a specific branch, build, commit, or pull request.

➤ **Related Work:** You can link the item to other items like GitHub issues and other work items. You can also create relationships between this task and others. Types of relationships include child, duplicate, duplicate of, parent, predecessor, related, successor, tested by, and tests (Figure 3.18).

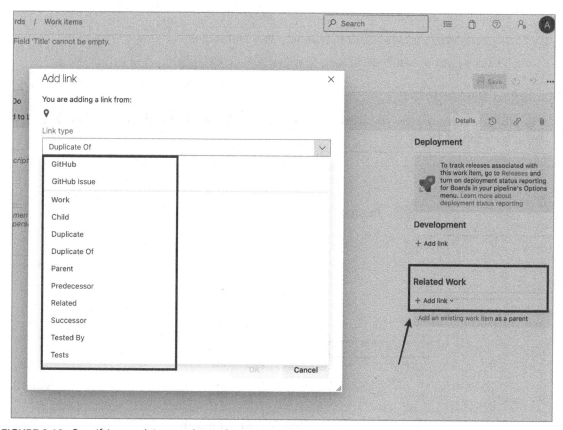

FIGURE 3.18: Specifying work items relationships

You have successfully created a new work item. I recommend creating a variety of work items such as issues, epics, and tasks. This will help you become familiar with the different work items and how to navigate them.

Backlogs

Backlogs help you plan your project with issues or epics. Once you have a plan, you can start working on writing the code for the product.

The product backlog is a roadmap of what your team plans to deliver. Backlogs have features that make project planning hassle-free. The following are some of these features:

➤ Quickly define tasks assigned to your team by identifying epics, product backlog entries, or issues

➤ Reorder your backlog to make sure you're working on the most important work items first

➤ Add details and estimates to your backlog items

➤ Quickly assign backlog items to team members and sprints

➤ Predict tasks to evaluate what can be delivered within a sprint

Managing Backlogs

The project dashboard gives you access to your backlogs. To visit the Backlogs page, select Boards ➪ Backlogs (Figure 3.19).

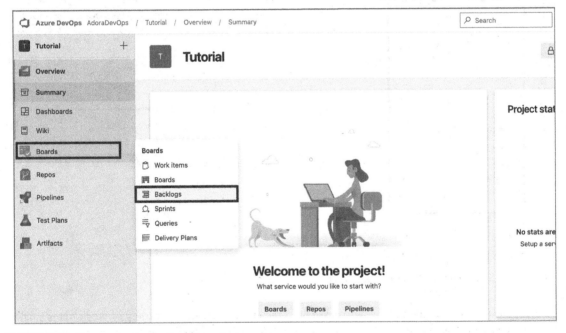

FIGURE 3.19: How to locate the Backlogs page

You can access your backlogs from your project dashboard. Select Boards ➪ Backlogs to visit the backlogs selection page and choose the backlog you want; this will redirect you to a page with a collection of tasks in your backlogs (Figures 3.20 and 3.21).

Here, you can see all other work items in the project (Figure 3.22). You can move work items into iterations (or sprints) from the backlog.

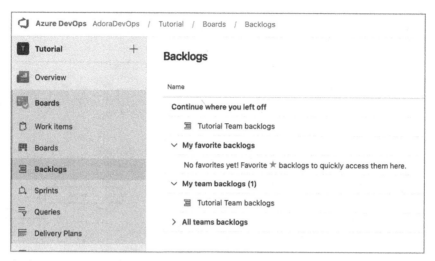

FIGURE 3.20: The Backlogs selection page

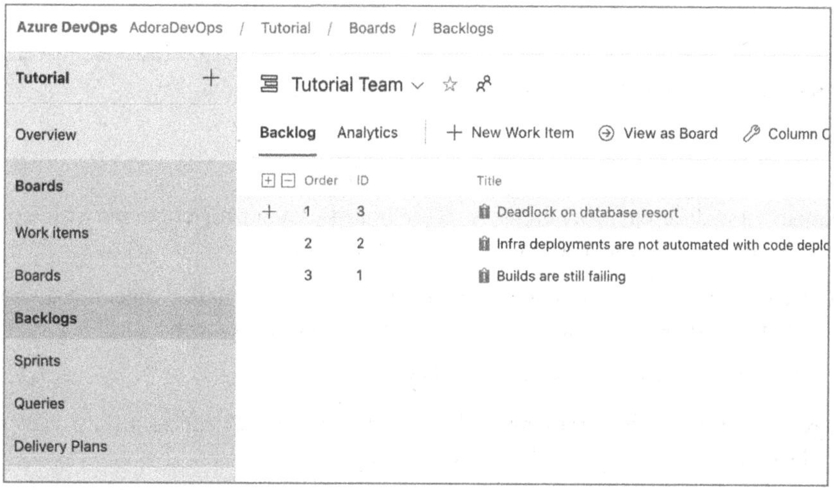

FIGURE 3.21: The Backlogs page showing a list of issues

In addition to moving backlog work items to iterations (or sprints), you can edit, reassign, copy, add relationships, or email work items. You can move work items between projects. This is especially useful when the organization is restructured and projects are reassigned to various teams.

You have now seen how to successfully navigate the backlog and move work items from the backlog to another sprint or project.

FIGURE 3.22: Moving work item to iteration (or sprint)

Boards

Another way to view different work items is to use boards. Each project comes with a preconfigured board that you can use to manage and visualize your workflow.

This board has several columns showing different stages of work. Here, you can get a complete overview of all work to be done and the current status of the work item.

Let's take a closer look at the boards in Azure DevOps:

➤ Select Boards from the left menu under Boards. Figure 3.23 shows an overview of the various works items added to the cards on the board.

Work items are displayed based on item status. The To Do column lists items that the team has not yet completed. And there are things that the team is doing right now. These are listed in the Doing column. When a work item is complete (writing and testing the code), it is moved to the Done column.

If you have not created any work items for this project, the board is empty. To fix this, go to the work items or Backlogs page and create all your tasks there. If you have successfully created a work item, it will appear here.

➤ During the life cycle of a work item, the status can be updated to Doing or Done, which can be done in two ways. The first method requires you to click the status of the specific work item you want to update and select the new status (Figure 3.24).

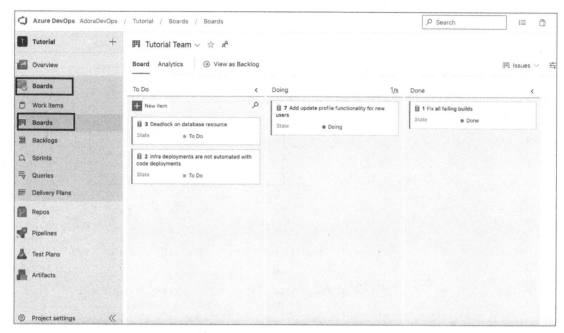

FIGURE 3.23: Azure DevOps project board

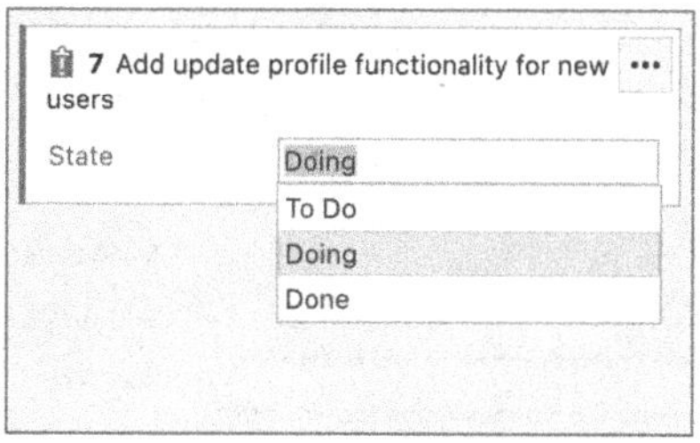

FIGURE 3.24: Updating work item status

After doing this, the work item moves to the selected column. The other way is to move the item by moving it from one column to another. This also edits the status on the card (Figure 3.25).

➤ To create tasks on an issue work item, you can click the three dots (. . .) on the top right of the card and select Add Task. Here, you can write a list of tasks needed to complete an issue. Think of the tasks like your to-do list. Once you complete a task, you can mark the task as completed by using the check mark beside it (Figure 3.26).

We have now successfully navigated through the Azure Boards features. I encourage you to play around with work item cards; you can edit them and move them across different columns on the board so that you can become more familiar with them.

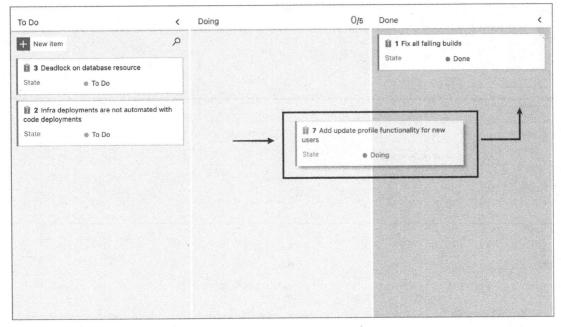

FIGURE 3.25: Dragging the work item from Doing to Done

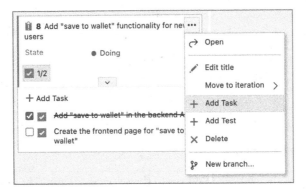

FIGURE 3.26: Create task from issue work item

Sprints

Sprints (or iterations) are used to divide the work into specific periods. Teams use two or three weeks for their sprints depending on what works for them. This is based on the momentum that a team can endure, that is, the rate at which the team is finishing the tasks.

Let's look at the Sprints page view in Azure DevOps in more detail:

➤ Select Sprints from the left menu below the dashboard. By default, the Backlog view is displayed. You can get an overview of the issues again here, except this time for the current sprint, as shown in the Figure 3.27.

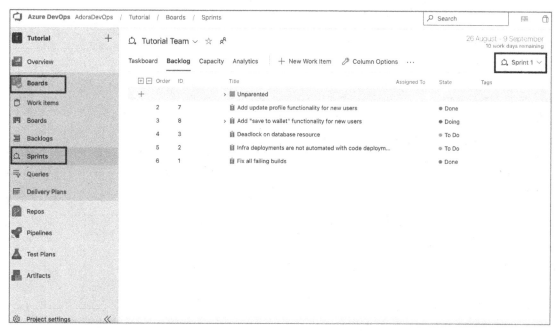

FIGURE 3.27: Sprint overview

The top right of the work items list shows the sprint name. In Figure 3.27, the sprint name is Sprint 1.

➤ Click Taskboard in the top menu to see different views of the work items in the sprint similar to what's happening in the board. This time, the items in the current sprint are shown at the task level in the backlog (Figure 3.28).

➤ From here, you can create new tasks under specific issues or in the unparented column; you can also drag, edit, and interact with work items as described in the "Boards" section.

Sprint task boards are often used by teams in their daily standups. Items are moved to different columns based on the team's progress. The team will also briefly discuss these elements and, if necessary, ask for help when there's a blocker or an error. At the end of the sprint, most items are moved to the Done column.

We have now successfully navigated through the sprints feature. You should play around with sprints by creating multiple sprints and moving work items around so that you can become more familiar with them.

Queries

You can filter work items based on filter criteria specified by Azure DevOps. This makes it easy to get an overview of all work items of a certain type, status, or tag. This can be done both within a project and across multiple projects.

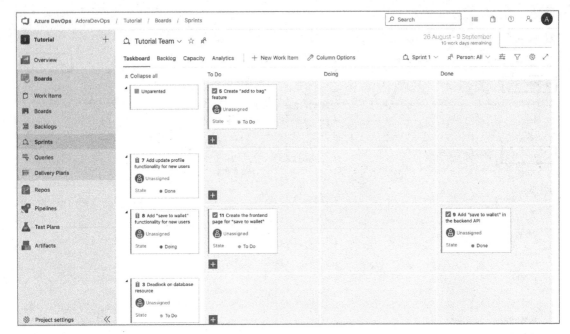

FIGURE 3.28: Sprint taskboard

To create various queries for searching through work items, complete the following steps:

1. Click Query in the left menu under Boards. Then click New Query from the top menu (Figure 3.29).

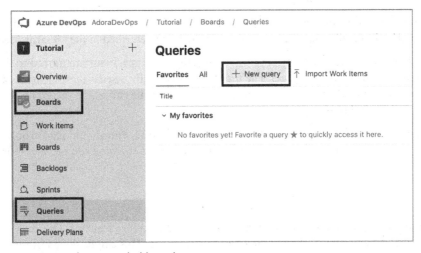

FIGURE 3.29: Navigating to the query dashboard

2.   Next, let's create a query that will be searching for an issue with the Doing state. On the query screen, select the options shown in Figure 3.30.

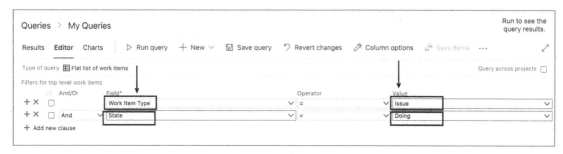

FIGURE 3.30: Creating a query

3.   Then, click Run query. The result will display all the issues that are currently active (Figure 3.31).

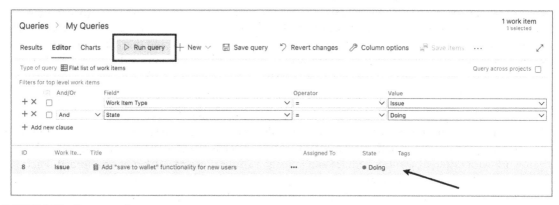

FIGURE 3.31: Query result

You have now successfully navigated through the queries feature. I encourage you to play around with queries by creating multiple queries for different work items so that you can become more familiar with them.

Plans

A delivery plan provides an overview of the work schedules of the different teams across sprints. This provides transparency between teams and helps administration make decisions based on outcomes and planning dependencies (Figure 3.32).

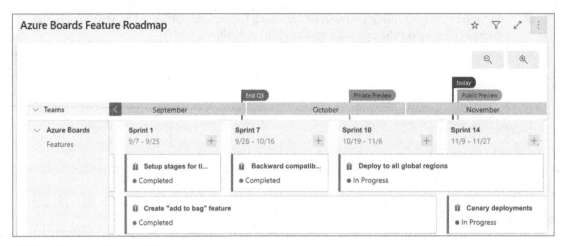

FIGURE 3.32: Azure Boards delivery plan

With delivery plans, product teams can plan specific milestones. Team members can have a holistic view of what they're working on and how their work aligns with the organization's broader goals of releasing or shipping new features to customers. Large software projects require multiple independent teams. These teams manage their backlog and priorities by themselves, and this helps the overall project direction. Regularly reviewing the project schedule with these teams will help ensure that the teams are working toward a common goal. Delivery plans provide the multiteam view teams need for scheduling projects.

For example, you can use a delivery plan to share feature schedules. By looking at what most teams have planned for upcoming sprints, you can determine if the plan has the right priorities. Therefore, the delivery plan is a coordination engine, and each team remains independent. Autonomous teams can work with different sprint schedules and manage various types of work items as needed. Their work can be seen in the same plan.

INTEGRATING AZURE BOARDS WITH GitHub

By linking Azure Boards with GitHub repositories, you can add links to GitHub commits, pull requests, and add issues to work items. You can use GitHub to write code while using Azure Boards to plan and track your tasks. Azure Boards provides the scalability to grow as your organization and business needs grow. In this section, you will learn how to connect your GitHub account with Azure Boards and verify that the integration was successful.

GitHub and Azure Boards Connection

You can integrate your GitHub Account with Azure Boards in these steps:

1. At the bottom left of the Azure Boards dashboard, click Project Settings and select GitHub Connections (Figure 3.33).

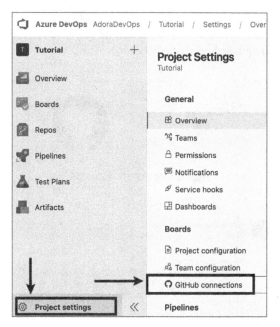

FIGURE 3.33: Project settings

2.   If it's the first time making a connection from the project, choose Connect Your GitHub Account (Figure 3.34).

FIGURE 3.34: Connecting to GitHub

Otherwise, select New Connection, and select your authentication method from the New Connection menu.

3. Follow the steps, and click Authorize Azure Boards (Figure 3.35). For security purposes, you might get a two-factor authentication prompt here. If you do, follow the steps to complete the authentication and authorization process.

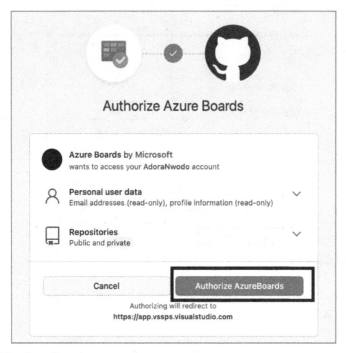

FIGURE 3.35: Authorizing AzureBoards

4. On successful authorization, you will be redirected back to Azure DevOps and asked to select the GitHub organization and repositories that you want to use with Azure Boards (Figures 3.36 and 3.37).

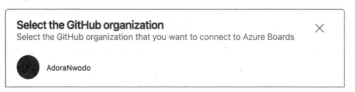

FIGURE 3.36: Selecting the GitHub organization

5. After choosing the repositories you want to use in Azure Boards, you need to approve, install, and authorize Azure Boards (Figure 3.38).

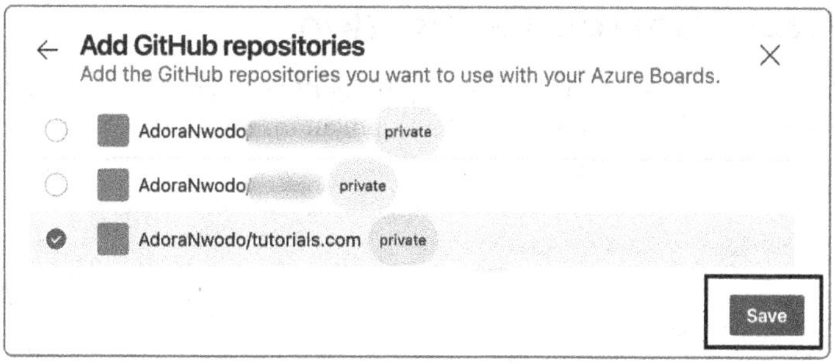

FIGURE 3.37: Selecting the GitHub repositories

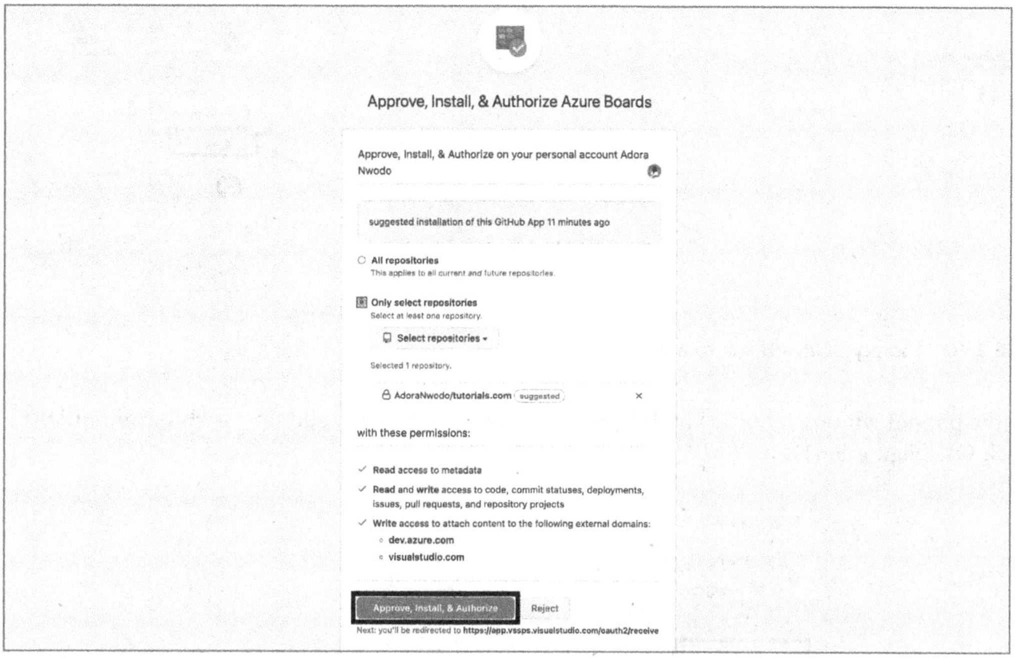

FIGURE 3.38: Approving, installing, and authorizing

If this was done correctly, you should now see a new GitHub connection in the dashboard. With this, you can now link GitHub issues, commits, and pull requests for the selected repository in Azure Boards (Figure 3.39).

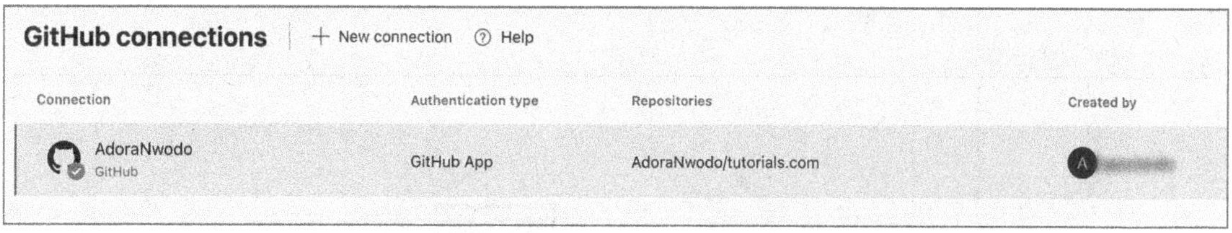

FIGURE 3.39: GitHub connection confirmation

GitHub and Azure Boards Verification

To verify that the GitHub connection works, visit any work item you have and try to link a GitHub commit to it. To do this, click the Add Link menu under Development on the work item, as shown in Figure 3.40.

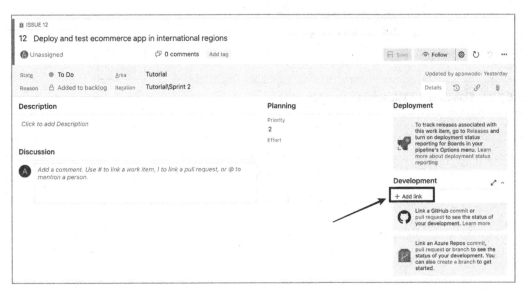

FIGURE 3.40: Adding a GitHub link to a work item

In the pop-up window, choose GitHub Commit as your link type, add the GitHub commit URL, and click OK (Figure 3.41).

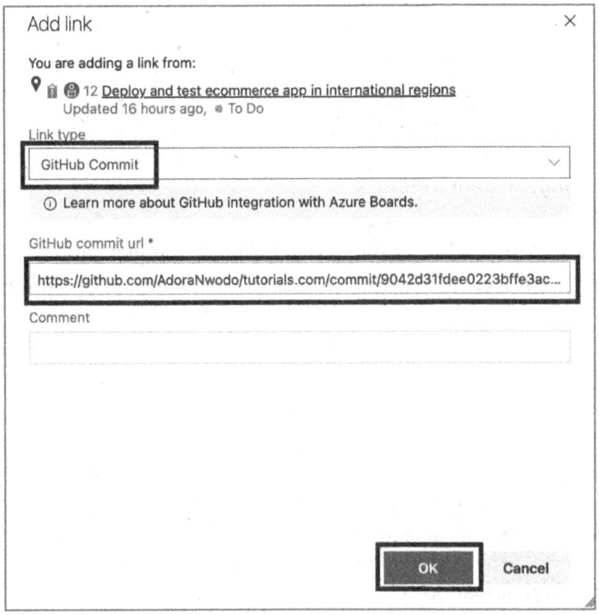

FIGURE 3.41: Linking the GitHub commit

After linking, the commit metadata should show on the work item's Development section, as shown in Figure 3.42.

FIGURE 3.42: Commit details

SUMMARY

Having your Azure DevOps organization follow a similar structure as your company is advised and simplifies the work planning process.

A single project allows teams to share source code, build definitions, code releases, and package streams, while multiple projects give teams greater freedom and granular security.

Basic, Agile, Scrum, and CCMI are all types of Azure DevOps project processes. These processes define the foundational elements of the work item tracking system used by Azure Boards.

Work items track all team's tasks by describing the requirements for a software development project. The product backlog contains various collections of work items. The backlog is the roadmap for tasks that the team intends to deliver. Boards aid the management and visualization of the workflow of software development teams. Sprints are used to divide and organize work over time. This is based on the speed at which the team does its work. Teams hold daily meetings to discuss progress and obstacles on each task. Queries are used to filter work items based on various filter criteria. This helps with searching and analyzing work items. A delivery plan provides an overview of the work schedules of the different teams across sprints. This provides transparency between teams and helps administration make decisions based on outcomes and planning dependencies.

Chapter 4 is a deep dive into Azure Repos. There, you will learn more about source control management using Azure Repos.

Version Control with Azure Repos

This chapter introduces Azure Repos and all its different features. You will learn more about source control management and how to use Azure Repos when writing source code.

What You Will Learn in This Chapter

➤ Version Control

    ➤ Version Control Systems

    ➤ History of Version Control

    ➤ Benefits of Version Control

➤ Git

    ➤ What Is a Git Repository?

    ➤ Create a Git Repository on Azure DevOps

    ➤ Import an Existing Git Repository to Azure DevOps

➤ Pull Requests

    ➤ Draft Pull Requests

    ➤ Create a Pull Request from Azure Repos

    ➤ Collaborate in Pull Requests

➤ Git Tags

    ➤ Annotated Tags

    ➤ Lightweight Tags

    ➤ Create Tags in Azure DevOps

➤ Summary

VERSION CONTROL

Version control is a way to track and manage changes to software code. It facilitates a smooth and easy path to software development. You can use the terms *version control* and *source control* interchangeably. A version control system is a software tool that allows software teams to manage changes to source code over time. Track all code changes in a dedicated database. As the development environment has grown over time, version control systems help software teams work faster and better.

Version control can be a single source and repository for product knowledge, history, and resolutions. Version control acts as a safety net that protects your source code from irreparable damage, giving your development team the freedom to experiment without being afraid of breaking code or causing conflicts (Figure 4.1).

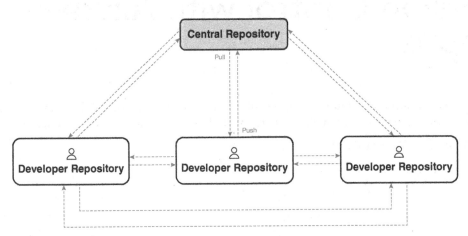

FIGURE 4.1: Version control

When developers make incompatible changes while coding simultaneously, version control allows team members to quickly roll back changes to previous stable versions, compare changes, or identify problem areas using revision history to find who created the problem code. A version control system allows software development teams to fix problems (e.g., conflicts) before they become problematic in the project. Code reviews enable software development teams to review previous versions to understand how the application has evolved.

Depending on a team's specific needs, a version control system can be local, centralized, optimistic, or distributed. In the next section, you will learn what version control systems are and see how these various systems work.

Version Control Systems

A version control system (VCS) is a system that tracks changes to a file or set of files over time. The most common type of version control system is a centralized version control system that uses a server to save all file versions. Software developers can check out the files on the server, make changes, and check the files back in. The server then saves the most recent version of the file. There are several types of version control systems, including the following:

➤ **Distributed version control system:** The distributed version control system is a type of version control system that allows users to access repositories from multiple locations. Software developers building many projects on various computers or working remotely with other software developers can use distributed version control systems.

➤ **Centralized version control system:** A centralized version control system is a version control system where everyone works in one central repository. This central repository can be on the server or the software developer's local machine. This system is often used in software development projects where development teams need to share code and track changes.

➤ **Lock-based version control system:** A lock-based version control system is a type of version control system that uses locks to control simultaneous access to all resources. Locking prevents conflicts by stopping multiple users from modifying the same file or resource at the same time.

➤ **Optimistic version control system:** In an optimistic version control system, each user has their unique workspace. Before sharing changes with other software developers on the team, the user will send a request to the server. The server then analyzes all the changes and decides which ones to merge safely.

History of Version Control

The evolution of version control can be grouped into three generations.

➤ **First generation:** The first-generation version control system was created in 1972. It was designed to track changes to individual files, and checked-out files can be edited locally by one user at a time. The version control systems in this generation were based on the assumption that all users connect to the same shared Unix host with their own account. A version control tool from this era is the source code control system (SCCS).

➤ **Second generation:** The second-generation version control systems were created in 1982. They implemented a client-server version control system using a concurrency model based on locking and merging. It led to a centralized repository containing the main version of the project. The centralized version allowed multiple users to view and work on the code simultaneously, so this was a welcome step forward. At this stage, software developers now also needed online access to commit changes. Examples of version control tools from this era include Concurrent Versions System (CVS), Apache Subversion (SVN), and Perforce Helix Core.

➤ **Third generation:** In the early 2000s, the third generation of version control systems came into existence, and we still use this generation today. It introduced distributed version control. The version control systems developed from this model are merge-based concurrency models that increase the overall history stored on each peer. Examples of version control tools from this era include Git, Mercurial, BitKeeper, Darcs, and Monotone.

Benefits of Version Control

These are the benefits of version control:

➤ **Collaboration:** Without version control systems, you would be collaborating on a shared folder on the same set of files. It is not an acceptable workflow to work on a file named xyz and shout across the office that your colleagues should not touch it at the moment. This process is highly prone to error. Sooner or later, someone else's changes will be overwritten. Version control systems give everyone on the team complete freedom to work on any file at any time. It allows you to later merge all changes into a common version. There is no doubt where the latest version of the file or the entire project is. It is in a common central location.

➤ **Backups:** The ability to restore a previous version of a file (or an entire project) effectively means one thing. If a recent change breaks your application, you can undo it with a few clicks. Knowing this will make you much more comfortable when working on your project.

➤ **Traceability:** Whenever you save a new version of your project, the version control system prompts you to provide a brief description of what changed. This will help you understand how your project has evolved between versions.

GIT

Git is the most widely used and modern version control system in the world. Git is a mature and actively maintained open source project, developed in 2005 by Linus Torvalds, the famous creator of the Linux operating system kernel. An incredible number of software projects, including commercial projects and open source code, rely on Git for version control.

Git has a workflow that can be summarized as follows:

1. Create a Git repository for your project.
2. Clone the repository to your local development machine.
3. Write code in different files in your local version of the repository and then save the changes locally.
4. Push the changes to the remote repository.
5. Pull the changes from the remote repository to the local one. This helps to align your code with the remote repository if other developers have made modifications.
6. Merge the changes with your local repository.

There are some important concepts in Git that you should know before we cover using Git in Azure DevOps.

➤ A *branch* is a separate version of your code repository. This represents a separated line of development. To modify the codebase, you should create a branch and work from there in isolation until you are ready to merge your changes.

➤ A *snapshot* records what all your files look like at a given point in time. This is a way to track your code history.

➤ A *repository* is a collection of all the different versions of a project and their history.

➤ A *commit* is a way to create a snapshot. It records the changes in the branch.

➤ *Cloning* is the act of downloading the contents of a repository from a remote server.

➤ *Pulling* is the process of downloading changes that don't exist on your machine from a remote repository.

➤ *Pushing* is the process of adding your local changes to a remote repository.

What Is a Git Repository?

A Git repository is your project's `.git/` directory. It is the same data structure used by version control systems to store metadata about a set of files and folders. This includes a collection of files and a history of changes to those files. This means that if you delete the `.git/` directory, the project history is also deleted. The repository contains all the data related to the project. Each project has its unique repository.

Create a Git Repository on Azure DevOps

Azure DevOps supports the following source control management types:

➤ **Git:** This is a distributed version control system and is the default version control provider in Azure DevOps when you initialize a new project.

➤ **Team Foundation Version Control (TFVC):** This is a centralized client-server version control system where developers have only one version of a file locally, data resides on a server, and branches get created on the server.

To create an Azure DevOps repository, there are some important things you should do first.

➤ Create an Azure DevOps organization and project. We covered this in the Chapter 3, and by now, you should have created yours. If you haven't, do that before moving to the next step.

➤ Get *Create repository* permissions. (This will be covered in the next section.)

➤ Get the Git tools. To install Git, visit `git-scm.com/downloads`.

Setting Repository Permissions

To set Git repository permissions on Azure DevOps, follow these steps:

1. Select Project Settings ⇨ Repositories and then click the Security tab (Figure 4.2).

2. Under User Permissions, you should see Azure DevOps Groups And Users. This means that you can assign permissions to groups or specific users, and the idea is the same (Figure 4.3).

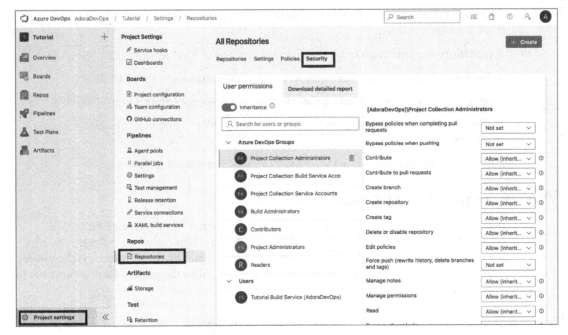

FIGURE 4.2: Repository permissions dashboard

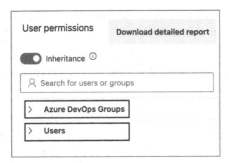

FIGURE 4.3: Types of permissions

If permissions are assigned to a group, all the identities in that group will have the ability to perform actions in the context of the permissions. However, if permissions are assigned to a specific user, only that user has access to perform certain actions.

3. Next, to set permissions for your account so that you can create a repository, type your email in the search bar and set Allow for the permissions you need. Figure 4.4 sets *Contribute to pull requests*, *Create branch*, *Create repository*, and *Create tag*. Depending on how your team functions, you can set as many permissions for different users as you'd like, but these are the repository permissions that you will need in this book (Figure 4.4).

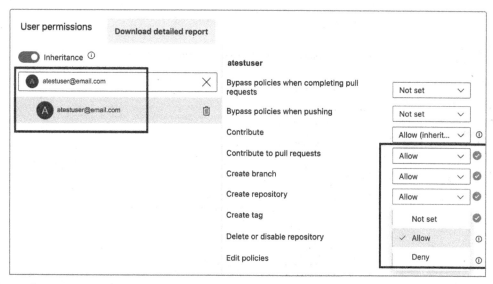

FIGURE 4.4: Setting repository permissions

4. Once you have completed these steps, you can leave the page. Your new settings are automatically saved, and you can proceed to creating your repository.

Creating the Repository

To create a Git repository on Azure DevOps, follow these steps:

1. In your project dashboard, click the Repos menu on the left sidebar. This will bring you to a repository dashboard, and if you've never created a repository before, your screen should look similar to the one in Figure 4.5.

2. From the repository drop-down at the top of the page, click New Repository (Figure 4.6).

3. In the Create A New Repository dialog, verify that Git is the repository type and enter a name for your new repository (Figure 4.7).

   You can also add a README and create a `.gitignore` for the type of code in the repository. A *README* contains details about the code in your repository. The `.gitignore` file tells Git which kinds of files to ignore, such as temporary build files from your development environment and environment settings. The `.gitignore` file in Figure 4.7 is for Node projects, but you can specify the particular project you'd like to initialize a `.gitignore` file for.

4. Once you have filled out the form, click the Create button, and you will have a new repository. Figure 4.8 shows what the new repository looks like.

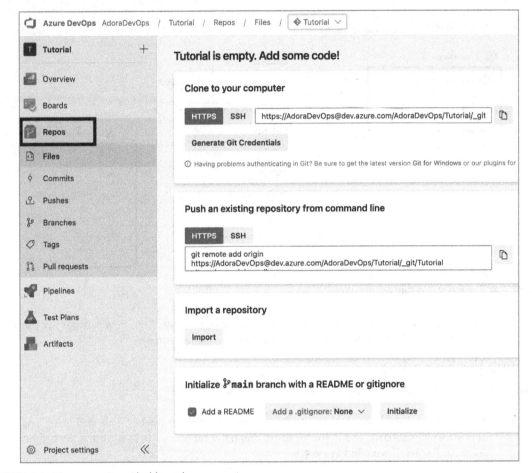

FIGURE 4.5: New repository dashboard

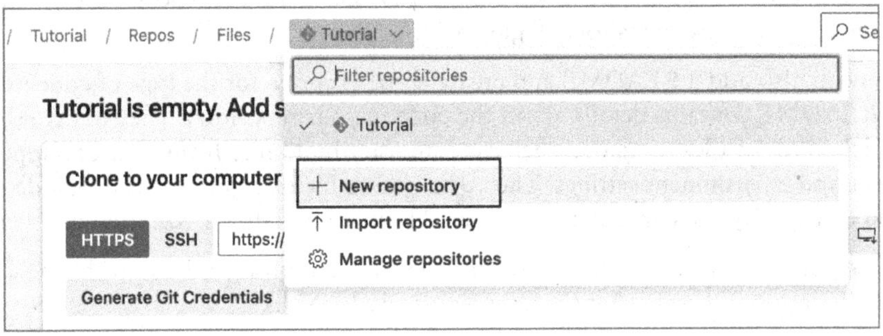

FIGURE 4.6: Clicking New Repository

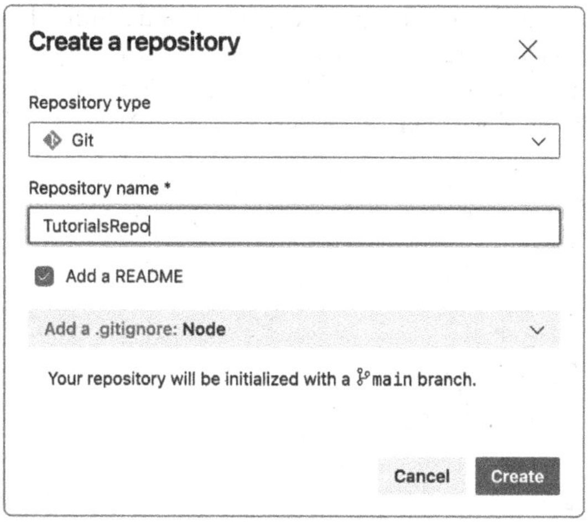

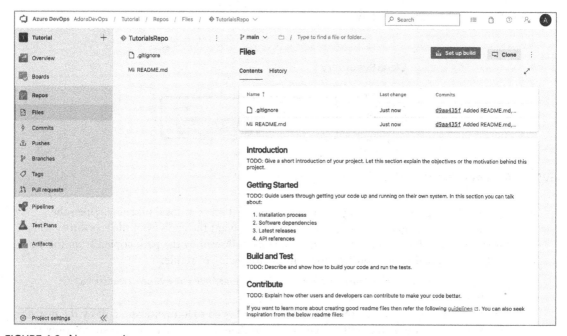

FIGURE 4.7: Create repository form

FIGURE 4.8: New repository

Cloning the Repository

To contribute code to the repository that you have just created, you need to clone it to your local machine. This section covers the steps required to clone an Azure DevOps repository.

1. From your project dashboard, navigate to the Repos dashboard by selecting Repos ⇨ Files in the sidebar menu. From here, you can select the repo you'd like to navigate to using the repository drop-down. In the repository, click Clone in the upper-right corner of the files window and copy the clone URL (Figures 4.9 and 4.10).

FIGURE 4.9: Selecting the clone repository

FIGURE 4.10: Copying the clone URL

2. This is the step that demands you have Git installed on your local machine. Open the terminal, and navigate to the directory where you want the code from the repository to be stored on your local machine. Run **git clone** followed by the path copied from the clone URL in the previous section, as shown in the following example:

```
git clone https://AdoraDevOps@dev.azure.com/AdoraDevOps /Tutorial/
_git/TutorialsRepo
```

If you are setting up Git for the first time, you will need to authenticate. Follow the instructions that show up on the pop-up window to authenticate so that you can successfully run Git commands.

Git downloads a copy of the code into a new folder for you to work with. The download includes all commits, branches, and other information from the repository. Once you've successfully cloned the repository, you can now start making code contributions.

Import an Existing Git Repository to Azure DevOps

With Azure DevOps, you can also import a Git repository inside Repos. In this book, you will import a repository from GitHub. To do this, follow these steps:

1. Click the repository drop-down menu and select Import Repository (Figure 4.11).

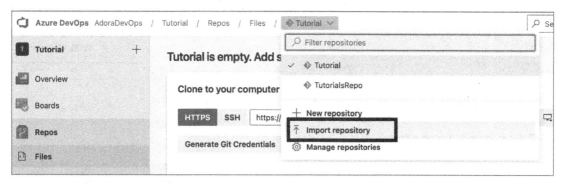

FIGURE 4.11: Selecting the import repository

2. A pop-up form for you to select the GitHub repository to import is shown. You can select the GitHub repository by entering the repository type (Git) and the GitHub repository's cloning URL. After that, choose a name for your repository and click Import (Figure 4.12).

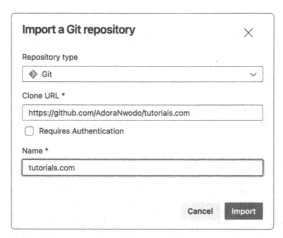

FIGURE 4.12: Import repository form

3. Once the import process has finished, you'll have the code available in Azure Repos. The code isn't the only content imported. As the repository is imported from GitHub, the history and revision information are also imported into Azure DevOps for complete traceability (Figures 4.13 and 4.14).

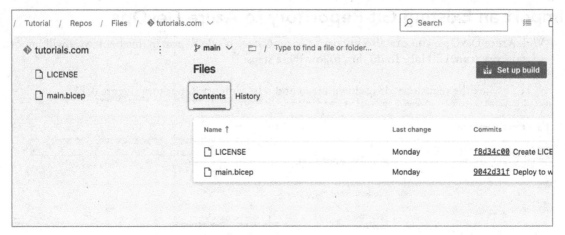

FIGURE 4.13: Imported source code

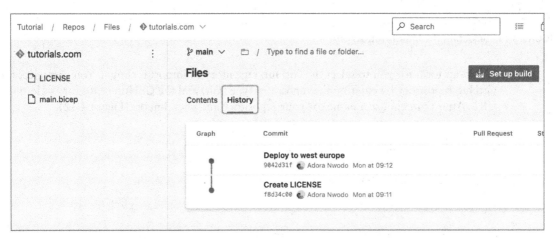

FIGURE 4.14: Imported repository history

PULL REQUESTS

Pull requests allow you to inform your team members that a new implementation has been completed and is ready to be merged into a specified branch. With pull requests, your team members can review your code, add comments about your modifications, and approve or reject those modifications. This is the recommended practice when using source control management with Azure DevOps.

Draft Pull Requests

A draft pull request comes about when you submit a pull request to make the work visible to others for early feedback even though it is not ready to merge. This is particularly important because you can get feedback and comments as you write code that's still a work in progress. During this period, no voting to approve or reject the pull request is allowed. Code builds and testing are also turned off during this stage until the pull request is fully published.

Create a Pull Request from Azure Repos

There are multiple ways to create pull requests in Azure Repos.

➤ You can create a pull request from the Pull Requests page.

➤ You can create a pull request from a feature branch pushed to your repository.

➤ You can also create a pull request from the Development tab in a linked work item in Azure Boards.

In this section, you will learn how to create pull requests using these three methods. You will also learn how to create and mark a pull request as a draft.

Creating a Pull Request from the Pull Requests Page

From the Azure DevOps website, you can create a pull request using the following steps:

1. On the Repos ⇨ Pull Requests page, click New Pull Request at the upper right (Figure 4.15).

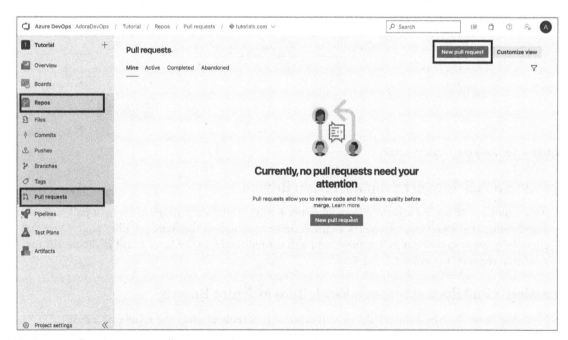

FIGURE 4.15: Creating a new pull request

2. Select the branch with the changes and the branch you want to merge the changes into. In this example, the branch with the change is called *new-feature-branch*, while the branch the changes will be merged into is called the *main* branch (Figure 4.16).

3. Fill the pull request form and click Create.

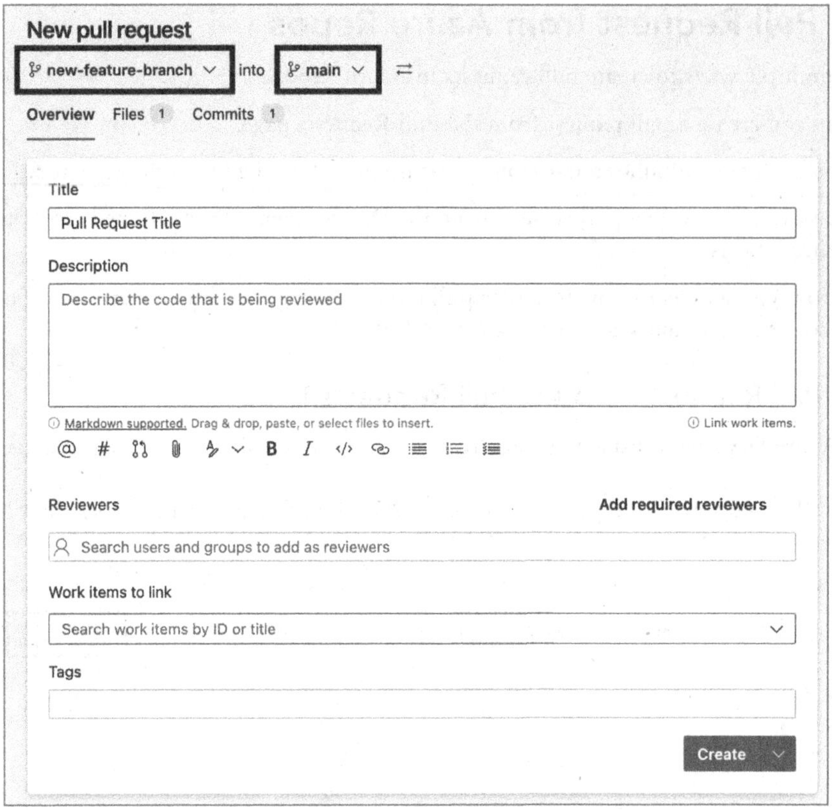

FIGURE 4.16: New pull request details

Creating a Pull Request from a Feature Branch

After you push or update a feature branch, Azure Repos displays a prompt to create a pull request. This prompt is shown on the Repos ⇨ Pull Requests page and on the Repos ⇨ Files page. Once you click the prompt to create a pull request, you will get redirected to the form to fill in the details for your pull request (Figures 4.17 and 4.18).

Creating a Pull Request from a Work Item in Azure Boards

From the Azure Boards dashboard, you can create a pull request using the following steps:

1. From Azure Boards, open the work item that is linked to the branch.

2. In the Development section of the work item, select Create A Pull Request. This will take you to the pull request page where you can fill in the details for the pull request (Figure 4.19).

FIGURE 4.17: Pull request prompt from Files page

FIGURE 4.18: Pull request prompt from Pull Requests page

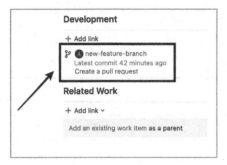

FIGURE 4.19: Creating a pull request from a work item

Creating a Draft Pull Request

You can create a draft pull request by using one of the three methods described in the previous sections. The only difference is that when filling the form to create the pull request, you select the arrow next to Create and click Create As Draft, as illustrated in Figure 4.20.

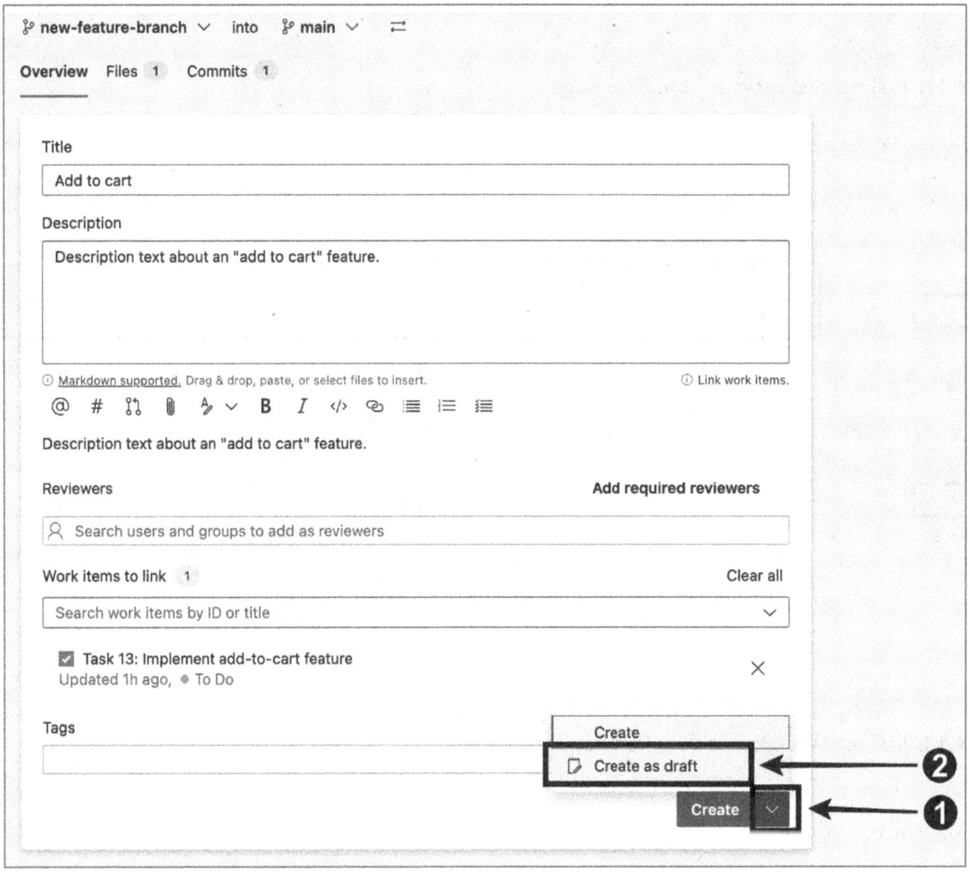

FIGURE 4.20: Creating a draft pull request

Collaborate in Pull Requests

Imagine you're completing a new feature in your software. You have already worked on the feature branch, so the next step is to merge it into the main (or master) branch. To do this, before you merge your code, you should open a pull request so that other team members can review your work and provide feedback (Figure 4.21).

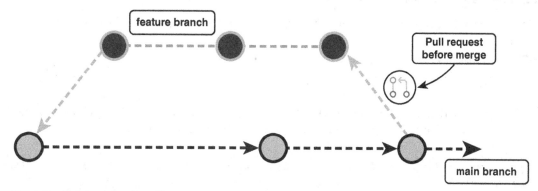

FIGURE 4.21: Collaborating in pull requests

When a pull request is opened, you can discuss the code with other developers. Azure DevOps allow other users to add comments and suggest changes during this process. Once the reviewers approve the pull request, you can merge the code into another branch.

However, having a code review culture on software development teams is not the only basis for a pull request. This is useful if you want to contribute to other repositories to which you do not have write access. Think of any open source project. If you have an idea for a new feature or want to submit a patch, pull requests are a great way to present your ideas without having to get involved with the project and the main contributors.

GIT TAGS

A git tag is a specific reference point in a Git history. You can specify a commit to establish a release point for a stable version in your code or future reference. You can include an unlimited number of tags in a branch or multiple branches. Git tags can be annotated or lightweight.

Annotated Tags

Annotated tags are stored as full objects in the Git database. This type of tag stores some additional metadata information, such as tagger identity and date. Annotated tags are also saved with the tag description. Azure DevOps supports the creation of annotated tags.

Lightweight Tags

This type of tag marks commits. A lightweight tag is simply a name or specific reference to a commit. Lightweight tags are useful for quickly generating links to related commits. To create lightweight tags, you can use the `git tag` command.

Create Tags in Azure DevOps

In Azure DevOps, you can create annotated tags from the Tags view or from the Commits view.

Using the Tags View

Follow these steps:

1. On the Repos ⇨ Tags page, click New Tag to create a new annotated tag. This will bring up a form so that you can add details about the tag you want to create (Figure 4.22).

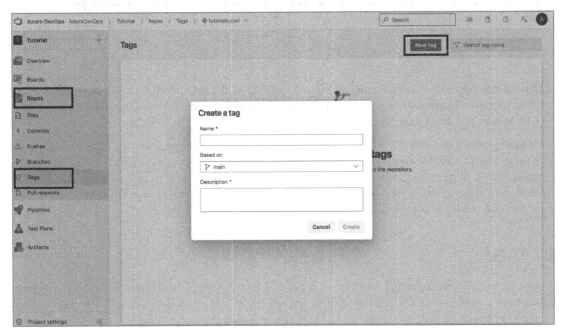

FIGURE 4.22: Creating a new tag

2. Since you are creating an annotated tag, specify a name; select the branch, tag, or commit to tag from; enter a description; and click Create. In this example, the tag is created from a branch called *new-feature-branch* (Figure 4.23).

3. You should be able to see your new tag displayed in the list of tags. Now, you can use this tag as a reference to this particular branch and commit in the future (Figure 4.24).

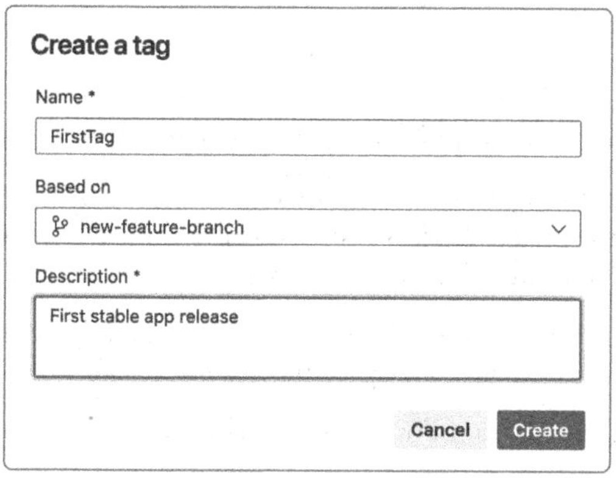

Create a tag
Name *
FirstTag
Based on
new-feature-branch
Description *
First stable app release
Cancel
Create

FIGURE 4.23: Creating tag form

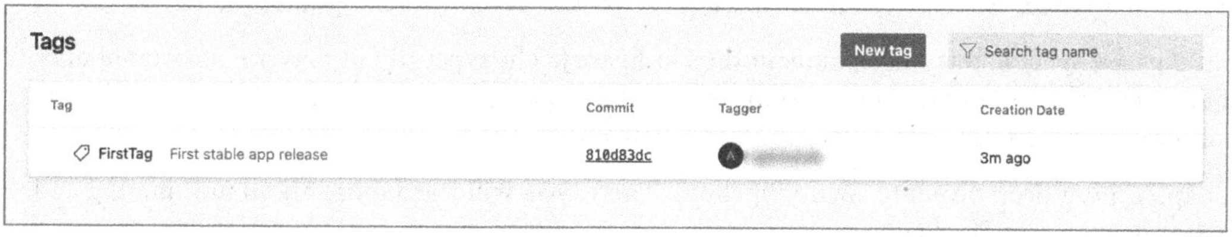

Tags
New tag
Search tag name
Tag
Commit
Tagger
Creation Date
FirstTag
First stable app release
810d83dc
3m ago

FIGURE 4.24: List of tags

Using the Commits View

Follow these steps:

1. On the Repos ➪ Commits page, switch to the branch you'd like to target, and you'll see a list of commits. From that list, right-click the three dots next to your desired commit. There, you will see a drop-down menu with different options. Choose Create Tag (Figure 4.25).
2. At this point, you will be redirected to the create tag form, and you can fill in the details as you like.

Commits
On
Commit ID
Graph
Commit
Pull Request
Status
Updated LICENSE
FirstTag
810d83dc
Sun at 19:40
Deploy to west europe
9042d31f
Adora Nwodo 29 Aug at 17:12
Create LICENSE
f8d34c00
Adora Nwodo 29 Aug at 17:11
Copy full SHA
Browse files
New branch...
Create tag...

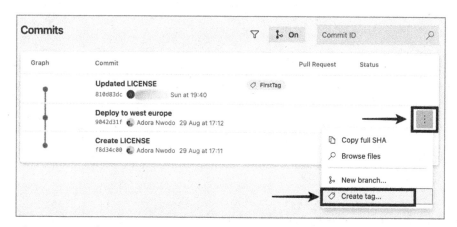

FIGURE 4.25: Creating a tag from commit

SUMMARY

Version control systems are software tools that help software teams manage changes to source code over time. It keeps track of every modification to the code in a special kind of database.

The types of version control systems are distributed version control systems, centralized version control systems, lock-based version control systems, and optimistic version control systems. Version control helps teams to collaborate better, back up their code, and trace work history.

Git is the most widely used version control system. It was originally developed in 2005 by Linus Torvalds, the famous creator of the Linux operating system kernel.

Azure DevOps supports Git and Team Foundation Version Control (TFVC).

Pull requests allow your team members to see your code changes and review them before you merge. In Azure DevOps, you can create a pull request from the pull requests page, from a feature branch, or from a work item on Azure Boards. Azure DevOps also supports draft pull requests.

Git tags are specific reference points in the Git history. The types of Git tags are annotated and lightweight tags. Annotated tags contain metadata, while lightweight tags are just a name for a specific pointer. In Azure DevOps, you can create annotated tags.

Chapter 5 is a deep dive into Azure Pipelines. There, you will learn more about automating code builds using Azure Pipelines.

5

Automating Code Builds with Azure Pipelines

This chapter introduces the continuous integration, continuous deployment, and continuous delivery processes in the DevOps lifecycle. Here, you are also introduced to some parts of Azure Pipelines, and you will see how to use this feature to automate your code builds.

What You Will Learn in This Chapter:

➤ Overview of Continuous Integration and Continuous Deployment

➤ Continuous Integration

➤ Continuous Deployment

➤ Continuous Delivery

➤ Overview of Azure Pipelines

➤ Azure Pipelines Features

➤ Defining Pipelines

➤ Components of Azure Pipelines

➤ Azure Pipelines Agents and Agent Pools

➤ Agents

➤ Agent Pools

➤ Using Microsoft-Hosted Agents

➤ Using Self-Hosted Linux Agents

➤ Using Self-Hosted Windows Agents

➤ Using Self-Hosted MacOS Agents

OVERVIEW OF CONTINUOUS INTEGRATION AND CONTINUOUS DEPLOYMENT

Here is an overview of continuous integration and continuous deployment.

Continuous Integration

The goal of modern software development is to have multiple developers working on different features of the same app simultaneously without conflicts. However, merging all source code updates from various branches in a single day is a tiresome and time-consuming task. This is because when a developer makes changes to software, it can conflict with multiple changes made by other developers at the same time.

Continuous integration (CI) helps developers merge code changes into a shared branch frequently, sometimes daily. When a software developer makes a change to the application and it is merged, those changes automatically trigger an action to build the application and perform various levels of automated testing to ensure that the changes do not break the application. When automated tests detect discrepancies between new and existing code, continuous integration can help you learn about those bugs quickly and frequently so that you can fix them.

Continuous Deployment

Continuous deployment (CD) is a DevOps process where application code changes that have been tested and validated are automatically released to the production environment in a series of steps and can be accessed by users immediately. Because preproduction pipelines have no manual gates, successful continuous deployment requires the tests written for the application to be well-designed and accurate.

Continuous deployment provides many benefits to teams that want to deliver quality applications quickly and at scale. It accelerates time to market by eliminating the lag between programming and getting the software to the hands of customers.

This makes it much easier to continuously receive and record user feedback. CI/CD approaches diminish software deployment risk by making it easier to release application updates in small fragments rather than all at once. However, this requires a lot of initial work in the CI/CD pipeline, as automated tests must be written and validated to enable the various stages of testing and release.

Continuous Delivery

Continuous delivery is another strategy for releasing software updates to production. However, this requires manual approval before every release unlike continuous deployment that automatically deploys to production when automated tests pass.

To achieve this, continuous delivery includes testing environments that mirror production. New releases from continuous deployment are automatically deployed to a testing environment that tests for multiple bugs and inconsistencies. These tests may include (but are not limited to) UI testing, load testing, integration testing, API reliability testing, etc. After the code passes all tests, continuous delivery requires human intervention to approve deployment to production. Then the deployment itself is done with automation.

OVERVIEW OF AZURE PIPELINES

Azure Pipelines is a cloud service from Microsoft Azure that automates the building, testing, and releases of software applications.

Azure Pipelines Features

Azure Pipelines has a lot of features, and some are listed here:

➤ **Pipeline syntax:** The steps and actions for CI/CD in your pipeline are defined using YAML. You can also define pipelines using the classic interface.

➤ **Programming language agnostic:** You can build, test, and release source code written in different programming languages and frameworks.

➤ **Operating system agnostic:** Azure Pipeline scripts can be run across Linux, Windows, and macOS machines.

➤ **Wide range of repositories:** You can integrate Azure Pipelines with different repositories such as Azure Repos, GitHub, GitHub Enterprise Server, Bitbucket, Subversion tools, Team Foundation Version Control (TFVC) tools, and other Git repositories.

➤ **Cloud provider support:** After building and testing your code, you can integrate different cloud providers and deploy your applications.

➤ **Versioning:** Like code, Azure pipeline runs are versioned. When you run a pipeline on a specified code branch, this can help validate your changes before you merge it to the main source branch.

Defining Pipelines

Using Azure Pipelines requires that you have an Azure DevOps organization and project set up. You also need a source code repository. It could be in Azure, GitHub, or anywhere else listed in the previous section. Azure Pipelines are free for some public projects but have a fee when using private projects.

In Azure Pipelines, you can create a build pipeline that tests your source code, and a release pipeline that deploys that source code to the specified target. Figure 5.1 illustrates the flow of the entire process from source code updates to deployment.

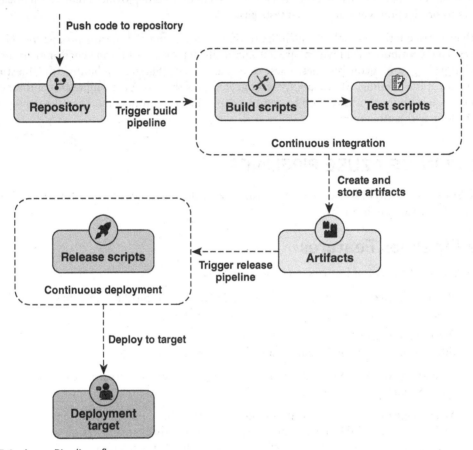

FIGURE 5.1: Azure Pipelines flow

You can set policies to automatically trigger your pipeline when you push code to your repository, or you can choose to run the pipeline manually. When the build pipeline is triggered, the scripts to build and test your code get executed, and if that process is completed successfully, the executables for your application (also known as *artifacts*) are created and stored in an artifact repository. You can also create a release pipeline that takes build output and publishes it to the target environment. Your targets can be staging, canary, production, or more. The destinations for these executables in the different environments can be virtual machines, web hosts, mobile application hosts, or more.

> **DEFINITIONS**
>
> **Target Environment:** *A set of resources that you can target with deployments from a pipeline. Deployments are usually done to these environments in stages, and rigorous testing happens before deployment to the next environment.*
>
> **Staging:** *A staging environment mirrors the resources and configurations of the production environment and is used to run automated tests and validate the quality of software before it is deployed to production.*
>
> **Canary:** *A canary environment is an environment where application updates that are available only to a subset of users are tested. These users test the changes, and upon acceptance, these changes get deployed to production and other environments.*
>
> **Production:** *A production environment contains a version of the application generally available to all users. Before application updates make it to production, they should be rigorously tested to avoid a negative impact on the end user's experience.*

There are two ways to define an Azure pipeline:

➤ The pipeline can be defined by creating a YAML file in your repository with all the steps you'd like to run.

➤ Azure DevOps also has the option for a classic editor. This allows you to select the tasks you'd like to run from a list of available tasks. Here, you do not need to write YAML scripts.

Defining Pipelines Using YAML

To create your first Azure pipeline using YAML, follow these simple steps:

1. Visit the Pipelines tab in your project dashboard and click Create Pipeline (Figure 5.2).

   That launches a wizard that allows you to set up your pipeline.

2. The next step requires you to connect your pipeline with a repository. Choose the location of the repository that you want to connect with your pipeline (Figure 5.3).

3. After choosing the location, you should select the particular repository you want to connect to (Figure 5.4).

FIGURE 5.2: Create Pipeline button

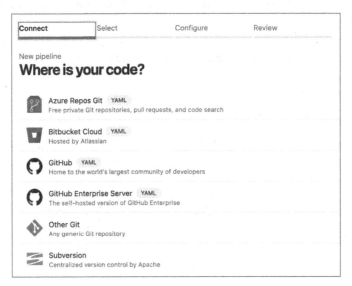

FIGURE 5.3: Connecting a repository to your pipeline

4.   Once you've selected the repository, you will configure your pipeline by creating the tasks that will run. If you don't have a YAML file, choose the starter pipeline to create one. If you have a YAML file in your repository, select Existing Azure Pipelines YAML File so that you can configure the file to run.

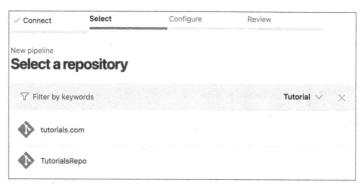

FIGURE 5.4: Selecting a repository

5. If you chose the starter pipeline, you will be redirected to a page with the starter pipeline YAML code, as shown in Figure 5.5.

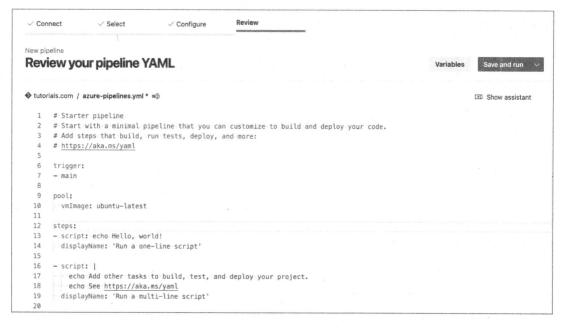

FIGURE 5.5: Starter pipeline

6. Click the Save And Run button. This will commit the new YAML file to your repository and trigger a pipeline run (Figures 5.6 and 5.7).

    If you want to run Azure Pipelines for free and your project isn't able to, you can apply for a free parallelism grant at https://aka.ms/azpipelines-parallelism-request.

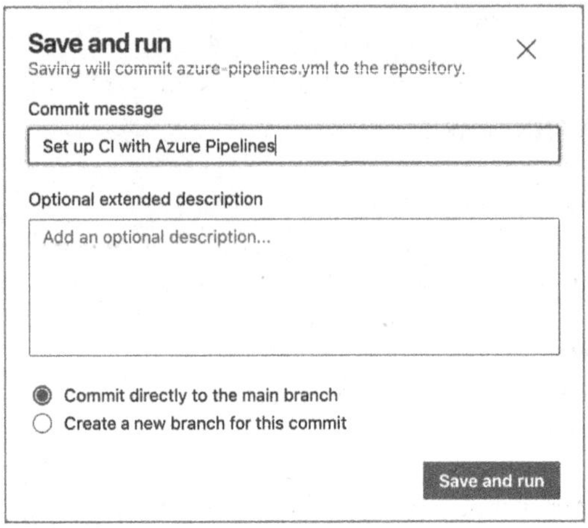

FIGURE 5.6: Saving and running the YAML

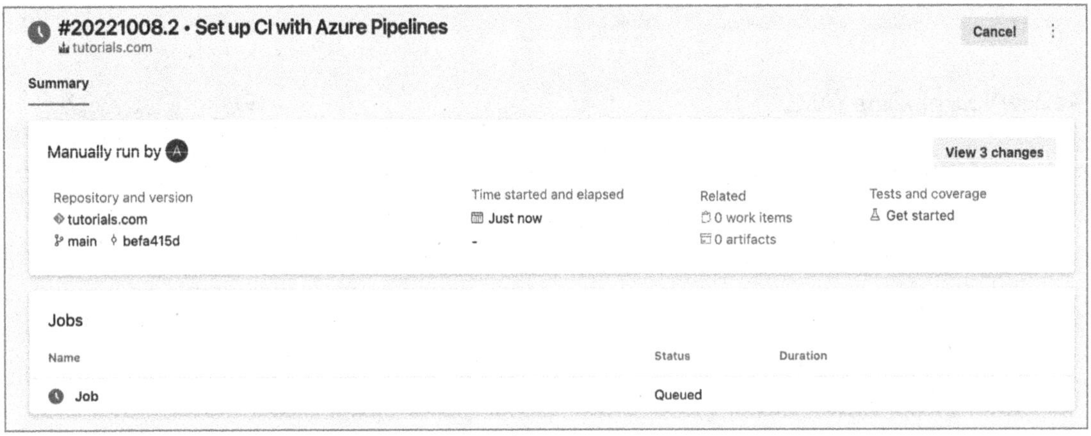

FIGURE 5.7: Adding a commit message

7. If you selected an existing Azure Pipelines YAML file, specify the file path in the pop-up window and click Continue (Figure 5.8).

You have now configured the pipeline, and it will run when manually or automatically triggered.

Defining Pipelines Using the Classic Editor

To create your first Azure Pipeline using the classic editor, follow these simple steps:

1. Visit the Pipelines tab in your project dashboard and click the button to create a new pipeline.

2. In the Connect Pipeline step, click Use The Classic Editor (Figure 5.9).

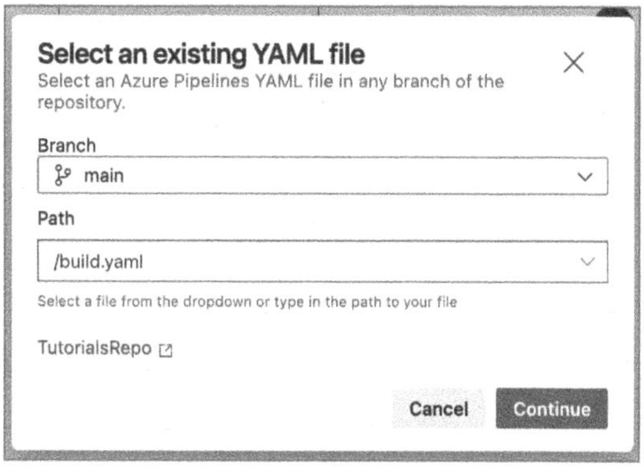

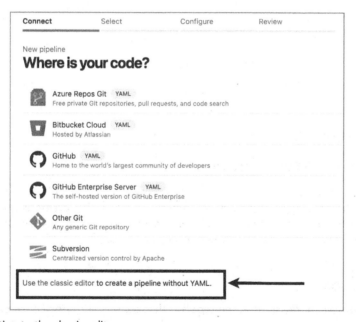

FIGURE 5.8: Selecting existing YAML

This will redirect you to a page that would allow you to configure the classic editor.

3. Specify the repository you want to create the pipeline for. After that, you will be able to choose from different featured pipeline templates (Figure 5.10).

FIGURE 5.9: Connecting to the classic editor

Initially, it might be easier to use the classic editor template. However, as you add more features to your pipeline and it becomes more complex, you will notice that YAML is more flexible and allows you to write more custom pipeline scripts that you might need.

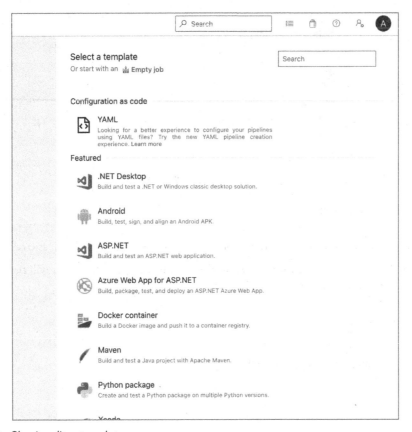

FIGURE 5.10: Classic editor template

Components of Azure Pipelines

A pipeline should consist of at least one stage. Each stage should have at least one job, and each job should have one or more steps. Every step is composed of a task that performs an action in the pipeline in the order the tasks were defined. Pipeline stages, jobs, and tasks are run on computers called *agents*. Agents can use either Windows, macOS, or Linux.

> **DEFINITIONS**
>
> *Stage:* Major divisions in the pipeline that consist of a specific set of commands to handle a related activity. For example, a stage could contain all the actions to test an application, while the next stage could contain all the actions required to deploy the application.
>
> *Jobs:* A series of activities that run in a sequence. Steps in a job don't run in parallel. The previous step has to finish before the next step can begin.
>
> *Task:* An action performed on the pipeline. An example can be a task to install dependencies on the agent before building and testing code.

AZURE PIPELINES AGENTS AND AGENT POOLS

This section will discuss agents and agent pools.

Agents

At least one agent is required to build and deploy code with Azure Pipelines. Agents are computers that execute the tasks defined in your build or release pipeline.

In Azure Pipelines, there are two types of agents you can define.

➤ **Microsoft-hosted agents:** This is the predefined agent provided by Azure Pipelines. These computers are fully maintained by Microsoft, so all you have to do is use them. You don't need to worry about upgrades, clearing the virtual machines, or their health. Every time you run a pipeline, a new virtual machine is created for each pipeline job. The virtual machine is terminated after the job finishes running. This implies that any change the job made to the state of the virtual machine (e.g., file downloads or checking out code) will be unavailable in the next job. Microsoft-hosted agents can be used to run jobs directly in the virtual machine or in a container.

➤ **Self-hosted agents:** These are machines that you create and manage by yourself. An agent can be a custom virtual machine in Azure or an on-premise machine that you own. Self-hosted agents can be hosted on Windows, Linux, macOS, or Docker containers. You can install the various software and dependencies required to run your pipeline tasks, and these installed tools will persist for each pipeline execution.

Creating a self-hosted agent requires doing the following activities:

1. Provision the resources and prepare the environment.
2. Configure permissions for Azure DevOps.
3. Download and configure the agent.
4. Start the agent.

Agent Pools

An agent pool is a group of agents. Instead of controlling each agent individually, you categorize them into collections. On configuring an agent, it is registered with the pool, and when you create a pipeline, you define the agent pool in which the pipeline will run. When you run a pipeline, it runs on agents in that pool that match the pipeline's requirements.

In Azure Pipelines, there are two types of agent pools that are provided by default.

➤ **Default agent pools:** You can use this type to register the self-hosted agents that you set up to run your pipeline jobs.

➤ **Azure Pipelines hosted pool:** This agent pool contains different instances of Microsoft-hosted agents running Windows, macOS, and Linux images.

To view the default agent pools on the Azure DevOps portal, go to Organization Settings at the bottom left of your Azure DevOps organization, and click Agent Pools (Figure 5.11).

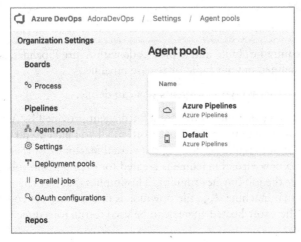

FIGURE 5.11: Agent pools

Using Microsoft-Hosted Agents

Microsoft-hosted agents are the most straightforward way to define an agent in your pipeline. The Azure Pipelines agent pool is where all the Microsoft-hosted agents exist. This collection offers multiple virtual machine images to pick from, each including a wide range of tools and software. The supported images at the time of writing this book are shown here:

IMAGE	CLASSIC EDITOR AGENT SPECIFICATION	YAML VM IMAGE LABEL
Windows Server 2022 with Visual Studio 2022	*windows-2022*	*windows-latest* OR *windows-2022*
Windows Server 2019 with Visual Studio 2019	*windows-2019*	*windows-2019*
Ubuntu 22.04	*ubuntu-22.04*	*ubuntu-22.04*
Ubuntu 20.04	*ubuntu-20.04*	*Ubuntu-20.04* OR *ubuntu-latest*
macOS 12 Monterey	*macOS-12*	*macOS-12*
macOS 11 Big Sur	*macOS-11*	*macOS-11* or *macOS-latest*

In the classic editor build pipeline, the default agent is the latest Windows agent, while the default agent in the YAML build pipeline is *ubuntu-latest*.

When creating a pipeline using a Microsoft-hosted agent, specify the virtual machine image name to use for the agent from the previous table. For example, here is the definition of an agent deployed using the latest Ubuntu image:

```
jobs:
- job: TestJob
  pool:
    vmImage: 'ubuntu-latest'
  steps:
  - bash: echo "Hello world"
```

The previous snippet defines a job called `TestJob`. This job uses a virtual machine with the *ubuntu-latest* image and prints *Hello world* to the console.

Using Self-Hosted Linux Agents

Linux agents can build and deploy many types of applications, including web, mobile, and cloud applications. It supports Ubuntu, Red Hat, and CentOS. The first thing to do when creating an agent is to register that agent in an Azure DevOps organization. To do this, sign into your DevOps organization as an administrator, and from the user settings menu on the top right, click Personal Access Tokens (Figure 5.12).

FIGURE 5.12: Personal access token

Here, you can create a new personal access token for your organization with an expiration date and custom access level.

WHAT IS A PERSONAL ACCESS TOKEN?

A personal access token (PAT) contains your Azure DevOps security credentials. PAT identifies you, your available organization, and your access options. Therefore, they are as important as passwords and should be treated with the same level of security (Figure 5.13).

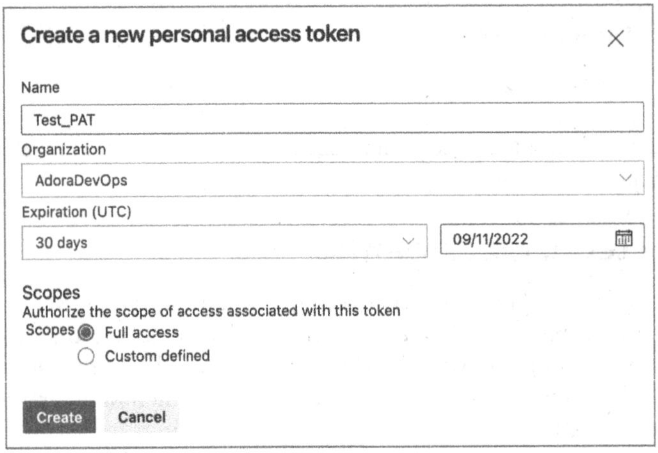

Create a new personal access token ✕

Name

Test_PAT

Organization

AdoraDevOps ⌄

Expiration (UTC)

30 days ⌄   09/11/2022 📅

Scopes
Authorize the scope of access associated with this token
Scopes ⦿ Full access
○ Custom defined

Create   Cancel

FIGURE 5.13: Full-access PAT

In Figure 5.13, the personal access token scope is set to Full Access. However, you can set the scope to Custom Defined and choose the different permissions you want. Keep in mind that you should set Read And Manage permissions for the Agent Pools scope in this step if you go that route (Figure 5.14).

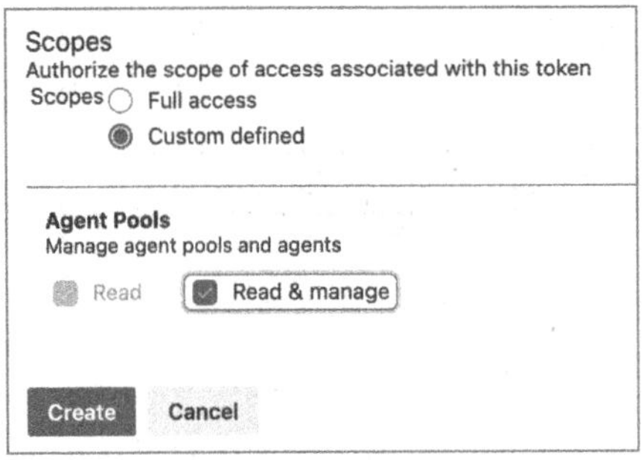

Scopes
Authorize the scope of access associated with this token
Scopes ○ Full access
⦿ Custom defined

Agent Pools
Manage agent pools and agents
☑ Read   ☑ Read & manage

Create   Cancel

FIGURE 5.14: Agent pool scope

If the Agent pools scope isn't visible on your current screen, you can click the Show All Scopes link.

After setting the permissions and copying your token, the next step is to visit Organization Settings ⇨ Agent Pools and create the agent. Select the Default agent pool and click New Agent; that is where you will create your self-hosted agents (Figure 5.15).

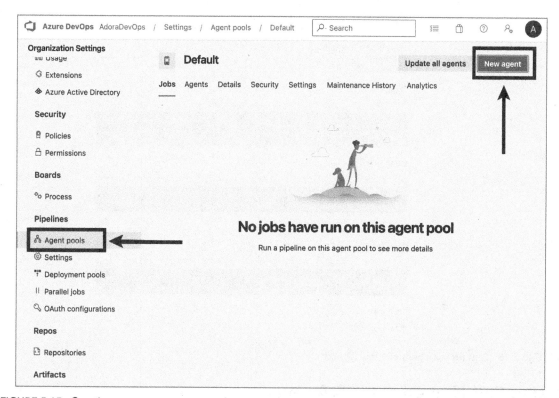

FIGURE 5.15: Creating a new agent

The Get The Agent window will open. Select Linux as the target platform, and follow the steps that show up (Figure 5.16).

Using Self-Hosted Windows Agents

Windows agents can build and deploy Windows, Azure, and Visual Studio solutions. They can also build other types of applications, including web, mobile, and cloud applications.

To do this, follow these steps (these are the same steps required in creating a Linux agent, so refer to that section if you want to follow step-by-step):

1. Create a PAT.

2. In the Default agent pool, click the New Agent button and follow the steps to create a Windows agent in the pop-up window (Figure 5.17).

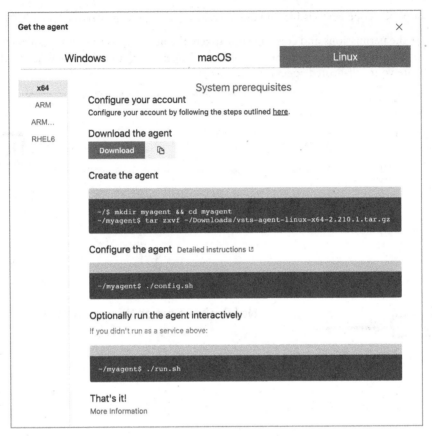

FIGURE 5.16: Getting the agent window (Linux)

Using Self-Hosted macOS Agents

macOS agents can build and deploy Xcode apps and Xamarin.iOS projects. They can also build other types of applications, including web, mobile, and cloud applications.

To do this, follow the highlighted steps (these are the same steps required in creating a Linux agent, so refer to that section if you want to follow step-by-step):

1. Create a PAT.

2. In the Default agent pool, click the New Agent button and follow the steps to create a windows agent in the pop-up window (Figure 5.18).

FIGURE 5.17: Getting the agent window (Windows)

AZURE PIPELINES BUILD SCRIPT

Azure Pipelines build scripts are YAML files that contain configurations for building, testing, and deploying source code when certain conditions are met.

YAML Overview

YAML is an acronym for YAML Ain't Markup Language. It is a human-friendly scripting language used for handling application configuration definitions. It can be considered a superset of JSON. Like JSON, the YAML architecture is based on key-value elements (similar to maps and dictionaries in regular programming languages).

```
- key: this_is_the_value
```

FIGURE 5.18: Getting the agent window (macOS)

YAML uses Python-style indentation to handle the configuration of the entity definitions, and it's insensitive to quotation marks and braces. It's simply a data representation language and is not used for executing commands like regular programming languages. When creating a YAML file, it's important to verify that your YAML file is properly indented and there are no syntax errors, otherwise your pipeline scripts will not run.

With Azure DevOps, YAML is crucial because it permits you to define a pipeline by writing scripts instead of using a graphical interface. The scripts can be shared and reused across different pipelines and projects, but the pipeline created using the classic editor can exist only within the bounds of the project it was created in.

Writing a Build Script

The following YAML script installs node and its dependencies, runs tests, and publishes contents of a Node.js app:

```
trigger:
- main
```

```
pool:
  vmImage: windows-latest'

variables:
  isMain: $[eq(variables['Build.SourceBranch'], 'refs/heads/main')]

steps:
- task:  NodeTool@0
  displayName: 'Install node v12'
  inputs:
     versionSpec: '12.19.0'

- task: Npm@1
  displayName: 'Install node packages'
  inputs:
     commands: 'install'
     workingDir: '$(System.DefaultWorkingDirectory)'

- task: PowerShell@2
  displayName: 'Run tests'
  inputs:
     targetType: 'inline'
     script: |
         echo 'Running tests…'
         npm run test

- task: PowerShell@2
  displayName: 'Build project'
  condition: and(succeeded(), eq(variables.isMain, 'true'))
  inputs:
     targetType: 'inline'
     script: |
         echo 'Building project…'
         npm run build
```

If you have a Node.js project, you can try this pipeline script and see what the result are. From the code snippet, you can see that this pipeline is triggered on the main branch and uses a *windows-latest* agent from the Microsoft-hosted agent pool.

We have also declared a variable called isMain. This variable checks whether this pipeline script is currently running on the main branch and returns true only if that condition is true.

As the first step to run, a NodeTool task is being used to install Node to the virtual machine. Azure Pipelines has custom predefined tasks that we can reuse instead of writing the actual scripts to do the work. NodeTool, Npm@1, and PowerShell@2 are examples of such task templates.

The next task is an NPM task that allows us to install the NPM dependencies required for this application to function. Next is a PowerShell task that runs npm run test, a command used to test NPM projects.

Finally, another PowerShell task is created to build the NPM project. This task runs only when the previous task succeeds, and the pipeline is being executed on the main branch. We can see this by looking at the *condition* on the task. When all these tasks finish running, then the pipeline is completed.

YAML SCHEMA DEFINITION INDEX

pipeline: *The different stages (one or more) that define the entire CI/CD process.*

condition: *A job, task, or stage should run only when a specified condition is met.*

jobs: *Specifies the jobs that make up the work of a stage.*

template: *A reusable pipeline script. You can define a set of jobs or stages in one file and use it multiple times in another file.*

parameters: *The runtime parameters passed to a pipeline.*

pool: *Specifies the pool to use for a job in the pipeline. A pool specification also holds information about the job's strategy for running.*

schedules: *Specifies the scheduled triggers for the pipeline.*

stages: *Collection of related jobs.*

steps: *Linear sequence of operations that make up a job.*

task: *Runs the specified task.*

powershell: *Runs a script in Windows PowerShell.*

trigger: *Specifies which branches cause a continuous integration build to run.*

variables: *Defines variables to use in your pipeline.*

variables.group: *References variables from a variable group.*

SUMMARY

Continuous integration helps developers merge code changes into a shared branch frequently, sometimes daily. When a software developer makes a change to the application and it is merged, those changes automatically trigger an action to build the application and perform various levels of automated testing to ensure that the changes do not break the application.

Continuous deployment is a DevOps process where application code changes that have been tested and validated are automatically released to the production environment in a series of steps and can be accessed by users immediately.

Continuous delivery is also another strategy for releasing software updates to production. However, this requires manual approval before every release, unlike continuous deployment that automatically deploys to production when automated tests pass.

Azure Pipelines is a cloud service from Microsoft Azure that automates the building, testing, and releases of software applications. It uses YAML for pipeline definition and can build software written in multiple programming languages.

Using Azure Pipelines requires that you have an Azure DevOps organization and project set up. You also need a source code repository. It could be in Azure, GitHub, or anywhere else.

Agents are computers that execute the tasks defined in your build or release pipeline. In Azure Pipelines, there are two types of agents you can define: Microsoft-hosted agents and self-hosted agents.

Microsoft-hosted agents are predefined agents provided by Azure Pipelines. These computers are fully maintained by Microsoft.

Self-hosted agents are machines that you create and manage by yourself. It can be a custom virtual machine in Azure or an on-premise machine that you own. Self-hosted agents can have Windows, Linux, or macOS images.

An agent pool is a group of agents. Instead of controlling each agent individually, you categorize them into collections.

In Azure Pipelines, there are two types of agent pools that are provided by default: default agent pools and Azure Pipelines hosted pool.

YAML is a human-friendly scripting language used for handling application configuration definitions.

Chapter 6 is a deep dive into automated testing. There, you will learn more about automating test runs using Azure DevOps.

Running Automated Tests with Azure Pipelines

"The bitterness of poor quality remains long after the sweetness of meeting the schedule has been forgotten."

—Karl Weigers

This chapter introduces the concept of automated testing, a very important step in the continuous integration process of the DevOps life cycle. Here, you are also introduced to different types of software tests. You will also learn about some parts of Azure Pipelines and see how to use this service to automate your software tests.

What You Will Learn in This Chapter

➤ Overview of Software Testing

  ➤ History of Software Testing

  ➤ Importance of Software Testing

➤ Types of Software Tests

  ➤ Unit Tests

  ➤ Integration Tests

  ➤ Smoke Tests

  ➤ Regression Tests

  ➤ End-to-End Tests

  ➤ Other Types of Software Tests

➤ Steps for Running Software Tests

➤ Setting up Testing in Azure Pipelines

➤ Summary

OVERVIEW OF SOFTWARE TESTING

When you build software, you and your team need to evaluate and validate that your software works as it should in the different conditions. This is called software testing, and it is an important part of the CI/CD process. As software developers, we are not immune to mistakes, and when they come up, a good testing pipeline allows us to catch them early to prevent bad experiences for customers who use our applications.

History of Software Testing

During the 1980s, software development teams began looking for a more scalable mode of testing as debugging couldn't scale for larger applications because it was becoming difficult to discover, isolate, and fix the bugs. The goal was to test applications under different real-world scenarios and expect that they behaved as they should. This was a turning point for how software applications were tested and validated as the software quality assurance process became part of the software development cycle.

WHAT IS QUALITY ASSURANCE?

Software quality assurance (SQA) is the continuous process of ensuring that software products conform to an organization's established and standardized quality specifications. SQA is a set of activities to ensure that everyone involved in a project follows all procedures and processes correctly.

Continuous Testing

Traditionally, software testing has been isolated from the rest of software development. It usually happened later in the software development life cycle or after the release phase of a product. The timeline for testing was timeboxed and never enough. Before product releases, if an error is found, there was a need to recode and retest. As a result of back and forth, software release deadlines were usually not met in scenarios like this.

Conducting software testing early in the software development cycle keeps testing at the front lines of software development rather than an afterthought. Testing software early means fixing bugs before the stakes become higher, which makes it cheaper. As a result, many software development teams have adopted a technique called *continuous testing*. The goal is to speed up software releases while balancing cost, quality, and risk. With this testing method, teams don't have to wait for the software to be completed before testing begins. As the software is iteratively being built, testing also happens simultaneously. This makes it easy for errors to be detected and fixed early enough.

Importance of Software Testing

There are many reasons why software testing is important as we build, and this section will cover those reasons:

➤ **Better customer experience:** The probability of bugs making it to the live version of the application that customers use is significantly reduced when software is tested. This improves the experience of your customers since they will not have to deal with navigating through a buggy application.

➤ **To validate compatibility:** Software applications run on multiple computers with various specifications. For example, browser-based applications run on the different types of browsers that exist, while desktop, mobile, and virtual reality applications also run on multiple devices with different specifications. Running software tests across different environments can help software development teams catch environment-specific errors and fix them proactively.

➤ **Security:** During the testing phase, the team can discover areas in the code that have security vulnerabilities. Some of these vulnerabilities include the following:

➤ The use of an unstable library that forces the application to be unpredictable.

➤ Unrestricted uploads of different file types without proper validation. This makes it possible for attackers to upload malware to your applications.

➤ Logging passwords and security tokens.

These vulnerabilities cause different risks in the application, and catching them early enough will allow the software engineering team to ship products that are more security compliant.

➤ **Better observability:** As software is tested and bugs are found, the software development team uses the logs, metrics, and traces to troubleshoot before implementing fixes. During the troubleshooting phase, developers are able to improve on the quality of the logs they have to gather more information about the application's behavior. This means that before the application is deployed to the version that customers use, the application will be properly instrumented so that the software development team can gather customer usage information.

WHAT DOES IT MEAN FOR AN APPLICATION TO BE PROPERLY INSTRUMENTED?

This means that the application is properly monitored (with logs, traces, and metrics), and software development teams can use the information emitted from the application to monitor or measure the level of the application's performance and to diagnose errors.

➤ **Application extensibility:** It is possible for a change introduced as a result of a new feature to break existing features of an application. Without testing, broken code will make its way to production easily. Testing promotes easy extensibility in applications because when the code that could introduce the errors as a result of a new feature is added, the tests will catch that bug, and the software developer can troubleshoot and fix accordingly.

TYPES OF SOFTWARE TESTS

There are many types of software tests, and each of them aims to achieve a particular objective. This section will cover the various software tests and what these objectives are.

Unit Tests

A software application is usually made up of different components, libraries, and functions. These different pieces should be validated in isolation to be sure that they work as they should when put in certain conditions. The act of testing the correctness of these components as a stand-alone item is referred to as *unit testing*. Unit tests are the most common types of software tests and also the most important for reasons highlighted here:

➤ Unit tests allow software development teams to validate the correctness of a small code unit. Usually, different test cases (scenarios) are written, and the goal is to confirm that the source code behaves in the way that it is supposed to.

➤ For software developers to write good unit tests, the source code itself has to be testable. This prevents multiple occurrences of *spaghetti code* in the codebase. Writing testable code allows software developers to write more modular code that can be extended.

> ### WHAT IS SPAGHETTI CODE?
>
> Spaghetti code is a generalized term for source code that is difficult to read and maintain.

➤ Unit tests allow software developers to test the modules that have already been completed without having to wait for the entire feature to be ready. This allows software developers to build and test their applications simultaneously.

➤ Good unit tests help other developers to learn about the functionality of the code and understand how to call already implemented functions (or APIs).

Integration Tests

After running unit tests, the next level of tests in an application are called *integration tests*. In this phase, software units are integrated and tested together. The reason for this is to expose flaws during the interaction between the integrated software components. In isolation, software components might work as they should, but bringing them together might introduce new kinds of problems the software developers need to fix before shipping the application (Figure 6.1).

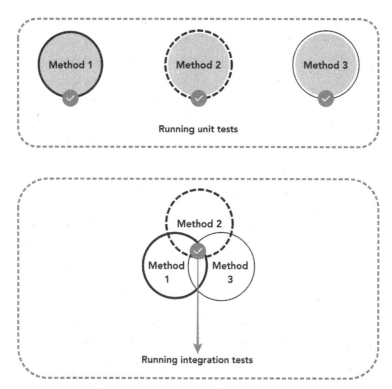

FIGURE 6.1: Unit versus integration tests

A CASE FOR INTEGRATION TESTS

Imagine a digital calculator application that has two methods: `subtract()` and `divide()`.

As a unit, the `subtract()` method performs like it should: it takes two numbers, computes the difference, and returns the result. The `divide()` function also behaves similarly. If we write only unit tests, we might not realize that combining these two methods in certain situations can lead to the calculator application crashing.

For example, if we perform multiple `subtract()` operations and one of the results is zero and we have to pass that result into the divide operation as the denominator, the application will crash in an attempt to divide a number by zero.

Integration testing helps software developers to figure out integration issues like this so that they can be handled gracefully without the experience of the application declining.

Apart from making sure that software applications work well when integrated together, there are other advantages of integration testing, such as the following:

➤ Since different components interact, integration tests can test and validate some real-life user scenarios.

➤ As features evolve, integration tests help verify that the application's core interactions are still as they should be.

➤ Integration tests improve code coverage and make the entire application more reliable.

Smoke Tests

Smoke tests are used to verify that all the important application features are working as intended. This is often an indication of whether or not the build after a code change is stable. If the build is stable, then the application can be checked into source control so that further testing and planned releases can occur. Beyond code reviews on pull requests, smoke testing is another cost-effective technique for finding and fixing software bugs. Smoke tests ensure that modifications in the source code behave as expected and do not break the build.

WHY ARE THEY CALLED SMOKE TESTS?

The term *smoke test* was derived from the hardware industry. The term comes from turning on an equipment after the hardware or its components have been changed or repaired. If there is no smoke, the component has passed the test (Figure 6.2).

Regression Tests

Regression tests are executed to confirm that modifications to the code do not affect the existing functionality of the application. This is to make the application perform better with additional features, bug fixes, or changes to existing functionality. In regression tests, previous tests are rerun to see the effect of the change.

A CASE FOR REGRESSION TESTS

Let's imagine your organization is building a social media application where people can post media and mutuals can react with different kinds of emojis. If a new feature request is made to add commenting functionality to the application, it can introduce new bugs and performance issues if it's not implemented properly because there is now more data to fetch from the APIs and load on the screen.

Regression tests allow software development teams to validate that this new added feature has not impacted the experience of the customer when they use other existing features, and if it has, they can catch and fix the errors before the stakes become higher.

The following are some advantages of regression tests:

➤ Like other software tests, regression tests help to improve the quality of the application, which helps users have a good experience as they interact with the software.

➤ The constant re-execution of tests helps ensure that old bugs do not resurface when a new change is made.

➤ Regression tests ensure that modifications do not impact the correct work done on the application and makes it easy for software development teams to detect and fix issues if they arise.

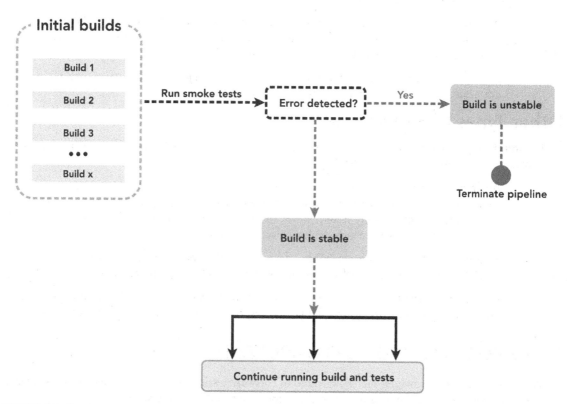

FIGURE 6.2: Smoke tests

End-to-End Tests

Today, technology is evolving, and applications have become more complex. Software is built using different architectural patterns on multiple layers and networks of subsystems, services, databases, networks, and third-party integrations. It has become important in the success of an application for the different application components to be reliable, because if one fails, the entire product will fail. This means that there is a clear need to test the entire application from start to finish at the different layers. Thorough testing allows teams to probe for new bugs and achieve high code coverage.

End-to-end testing is a methodology software development teams use to test the different layers of their application. It tests the functionality and performance of an application under product-like circumstances and data to imitate live scenarios. The objective is to emulate what a real customer scenario would look like from start to finish. Completing these tests not only verifies the system under test but also ensures that the subsystems are working and operating as expected.

End-to-end tests are more reliable and widely used due to the following advantages:

➤ End-to-end testing ensures that your software works at all layers, from application interface to backend (APIs), and across multiple systems. It also provides insights into performance metrics in different application environments.

➤ With end-to-end testing, applications are typically tested after each iteration, allowing you to find and fix problems faster. This reduces the likelihood of bugs finding their way into production, ensuring the application works as it should.

➤ By testing across multiple layers, you will be able to add additional test cases that might have not been considered in unit and integration tests.

Other Types of Software Tests

Beyond the types of software tests already mentioned in previous sections, there are other ways that you can test your applications.

➤ **Acceptance tests:** Acceptance testing (also known as *user acceptance testing*) is a type of testing where the customer tests the software with real-time business scenarios. The customer accepts the application only if all features work as planned. This is the final testing phase after which the application gets deployed into production.

➤ **Security tests:** Security tests verify how the application handles threats. Security tests also check how the application behaves in the event of a hacker or malware attack.

➤ **Performance tests:** Performance testing is a software testing technique that determines how an application's stability, speed, scalability, and responsiveness perform under a given workload.

STEPS FOR RUNNING SOFTWARE TESTS

Previous sections have covered the background of software testing and the different kinds of software tests that exist. To run these tests in Azure, it is important to follow these steps:

➤ **Create a test plan:** A test plan is a detailed document that describes the software test strategy, goals, schedule, required resources, estimation, and results. The test plan is the foundation for testing any software. It is the most significant activity that guarantees that all the expected test tasks are defined.

➤ **Create test cases:** A test case is a collection of actions performed to validate a specific aspect of an application's functionality. If the test fails, the result could be a software defect that the software development team needs to fix.

➤ **Execute tests and record results:** After creating the tests, run the tests to determine what the outcome on the application is. Record results where necessary (e.g., when running performance tests).

➤ **Fix test errors:** If there were errors during any test execution, it means that the application should not be deployed to production yet. Software development teams can take some time to troubleshoot, identify, and fix the errors.

SETTING UP TESTING IN AZURE PIPELINES

In Azure Pipelines, you can run tests for .NET Core, Python, Android (Java and Kotlin), ASP.NET, C, C++, Go, PHP, Ruby, Xamarin, Xcode, JavaScript, and Node.js. In this section, you will see how to set up Azure Pipelines for automated testing.

> **DEFINITION** *Terms Used in Azure Pipelines Tests*
>
> **Duration:** *The time taken to run tests in a build or release pipeline*
>
> **Failing build:** *A build pipeline with at least one test case that has errors*
>
> **Failing release:** *A release pipeline with at least one test case that has errors*
>
> **Flaky tests:** *A test with nondeterministic behavior. For example, testing may have different results for the same configuration, code, or inputs*
>
> **Test case:** *Uniquely specifies a single test that can be executed within the specified codebase*
>
> **Test report:** *A view of a single instance of test execution in the pipeline that contains details of the status and helps debugging, traceability, and more*
>
> **Test result:** *Single execution instance of a test case with a specific result and details*
>
> **Traceability:** *Ability to trace to a requirement, bug, or source code from a test result*

To run a test in Azure Pipelines, you should have the following prerequisites:

➤ An Azure DevOps organization

➤ An application with tests that are written in any of the supported languages or frameworks for Azure

Now, let's get started.

➤ In your Azure DevOps project dashboard, create a new pipeline.

Click Use The Classic Editor. . . so that you can create a pipeline without YAML (Figure 6.3).

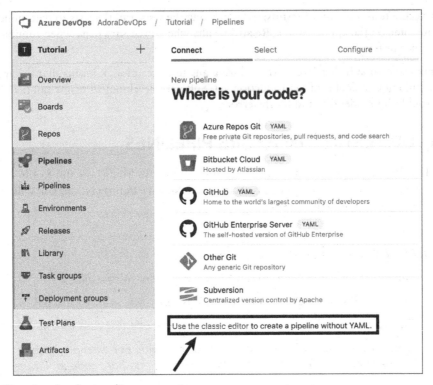

FIGURE 6.3: Choosing the classic editor

Then follow these steps:

1. Select the source of your project. It could be Azure Repos, GitHub, GitHub Enterprise Server, Subversion, Bitbucket, or any other supported Git repository. Note that you will have to authenticate to import projects outside of Azure Repos. In Figure 6.4, the source is Azure Repos Git.

2. Once you select your pipeline source, click Continue.

3. Choose a template for your pipeline. This template should be in sync with the programming language (or library) for your project. Figure 6.5 shows using an ASP.NET template, but you can choose the right template for your own project. Azure has a wide range to choose from, so scroll and select the suitable template.

    If you don't find a template that works for you, you can create a YAML template, as shown in Figure 6.6.

4. After choosing your template, you will be able to see the proposed tasks that will be created when your pipeline gets created. In ASP.NET, one of these tasks is Test Assemblies. This task contains step-by-step actions for running tests against ASP.NET projects (Figure 6.7).

FIGURE 6.4: Selecting a pipeline source

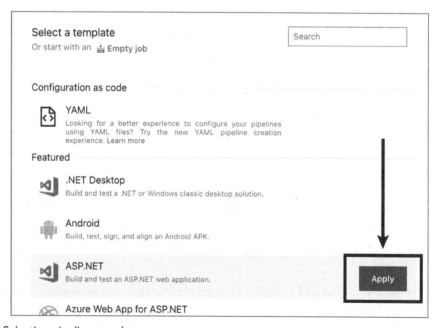

FIGURE 6.5: Selecting pipeline templates

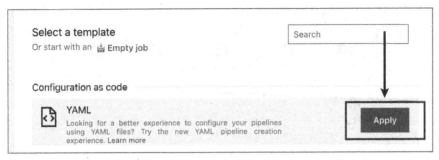

FIGURE 6.6: Selecting YAML (Default)

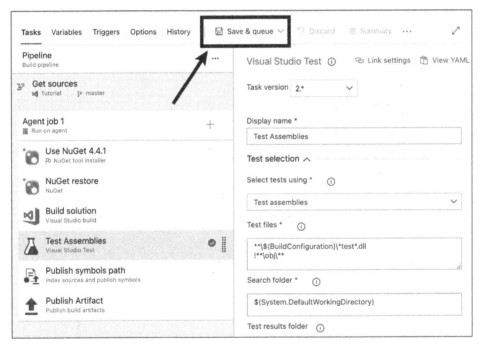

FIGURE 6.7: Build tasks

5. You can edit any of the fields you deem fit before you hit the Save & Queue button.

6. Once you save and queue, a form to select parameters for the pipeline will pop up. You can edit this as you like based on what your requirements are, and then click Save And Run (Figure 6.8).

You have now successfully created an ASP.NET build pipeline that runs automated tests. Once the build is complete, you will be able to see the test results in your pipeline. Your build and test results page will look similar to Figure 6.9.

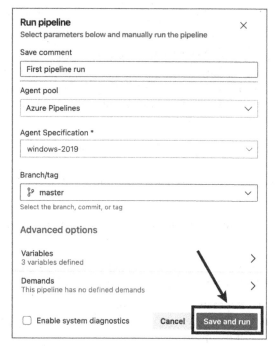

FIGURE 6.8: Running a pipeline form

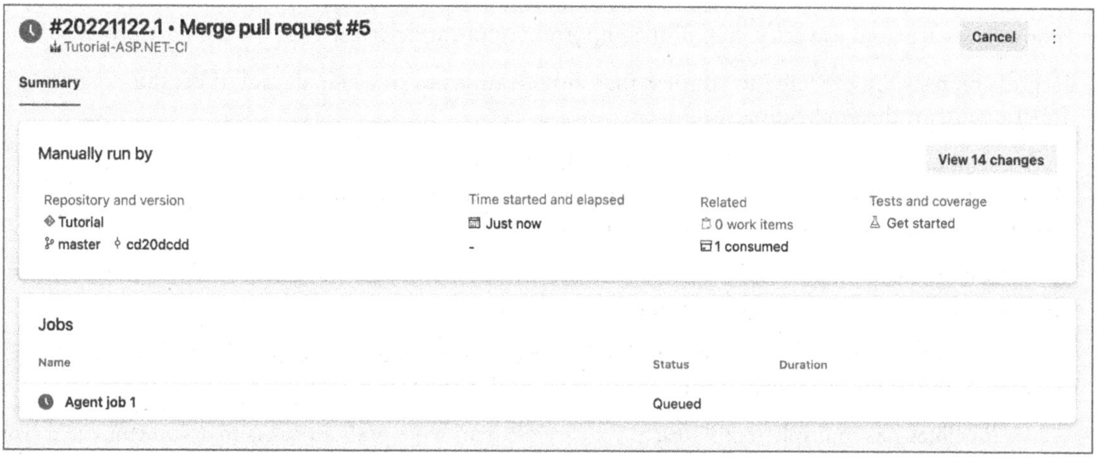

FIGURE 6.9: Build and test results

PRACTICE WORK

In this section, you set up an ASP.NET test in Azure Pipelines. You can decide to extend this example by adding more tests and pipeline stages. You can also try to do this beyond ASP.NET. If you have a project in Python, Java, Xcode, or any other supported platform, add it to Azure Pipelines and run automated tests for it.

SUMMARY

Software testing is a technique used to validate that applications work as they should.

Software testing is important because it promotes a better customer experience and better security while making sure that applications are compatible across different platforms and that source code can be extended.

There are many kinds of software tests. Some of them are unit tests, integration tests, smoke tests, regression tests, and end-to-end tests.

Unit tests allow software development teams to validate the correctness of a small code unit in isolation. Usually, different test cases (scenarios) are written, and the goal is to confirm that the source code behaves in the way that it is supposed to.

In integration tests, software units are integrated and tested together. The reason for this is to expose flaws during the interaction between the integrated software components.

Smoke tests are used to verify that all the important application features are working as intended.

Regression tests are executed to confirm that modifications to the code do not affect the existing functionality of the application.

End-to-end testing is a methodology software development teams use to test the different layers of their application. It tests the functionality and performance of an application under product-like circumstances and data to imitate live scenarios.

In the software testing process, you should create a test plan, create test cases, execute your test, and fix issues that come up to make your application better.

In Azure Pipelines, you can run tests for .NET Core, Python, Android (Java and Kotlin), ASP.NET, C, C++, Go, PHP, Ruby, Xamarin, Xcode, JavaScript, and Node.js.

Azure Pipelines has multiple templates, and many of them have prebuilt tasks that you can use to run your automated tests in the pipeline.

Chapter 7 is a deep dive into Azure Artifacts. There you will learn about Azure Artifacts and how to use it to manage your source code packages.

7

Creating and Hosting Source Code Packages with Azure Artifacts

This chapter covers Azure Artifacts. Here you will learn about Azure Artifacts and how to use it to manage your source code packages.

What You Will Learn in This Chapter

➤ Overview of Artifact Repositories

➤ Introduction to Azure Artifacts

➤ Azure Artifact Feeds

   ➤ Project-Scoped Feeds

   ➤ Organizational-Scoped Feeds

   ➤ How to Create an Azure Artifacts Feed

   ➤ Public Feeds

➤ Azure Artifact Feed Views

   ➤ Types of Azure Artifacts Feed Views

➤ Upstream Sources

   ➤ Setting Up Upstream Sources

➤ Publishing Artifacts in Azure Pipelines

   ➤ Publishing Artifacts Using the Publish Keyword in YAML

   ➤ Publishing Artifacts Using a YAML Task

   ➤ Publishing Artifacts Using the Classic Editor

➤ Downloading Artifacts in Azure Pipelines

    ➤ Downloading Artifacts Using the Download Keyword in YAML

    ➤ Downloading Artifacts Using a YAML Task

    ➤ Downloading Artifacts Using the Classic Editor

➤ Summary

OVERVIEW OF ARTIFACT REPOSITORIES

As a software developer, you have probably imported and used an open-source package in one of your projects to prevent you from reinventing the wheel. These packages were created and published by other people who want to share code. Some shared packages are utility libraries, while others are frameworks for software development that can be used across different programming languages. Importing shared source code requires that the code be stored somewhere for people to gain access to it. The stored location is called an *artifact repository*.

An *artifact* is a deployable component of your application. The primary purpose of an artifact repository is to securely store artifacts that are created during the software development process. These artifacts can be packages that other software developers can use across different organizations, but they can also be binary output from the continuous integration process in the CI/CD pipeline. Artifact repositories store two kinds of artifacts: build artifacts and deployment artifacts.

➤ **Build artifacts:** These artifacts are the outputs of the continuous integration step in your pipeline. They exist only in the context of your pipeline. When the build step runs, source code binaries (also known as *artifacts*) are created and published to a path on the active virtual machine running the pipeline. These binaries are then used for testing and other validation checks that run within the pipeline.

➤ **Deployment artifacts:** These are executables that are released for the public to use. They are generated during the deployment stage of the pipeline. Releasing deployment artifacts requires more security and versioning, since these are the packages that many people import and use in their projects.

INTRODUCTION TO AZURE ARTIFACTS

Azure has an artifacts repository included as part of its Azure DevOps Services. With Azure Artifacts, you can share your code effectively and organize all your packages from a central location.

Azure Artifacts supports several types of packages, including NuGet, npm, Python, Maven, and universal packages. Build artifacts and symbols are also supported within Azure Artifacts. It also allows software developers to publish packages and share them in different ways.

➤ Internally with their teams

➤ Within the organization but outside the team

➤ To the general public

> ### WHAT ARE SYMBOLS?
>
> *Symbols* are files that contain debugging information for compiled binaries. Azure Artifacts has a symbols server to which software developers can also publish their symbol files.

AZURE ARTIFACTS FEEDS

An Azure Artifacts feed is a cloud-based location where you can keep and organize software packages. Artifact feeds are not unique to the type of package. Different packages such as npm, NuGet, Maven, Python, and universal packages can exist on the same artifact feed.

For the sake of visibility, Azure Artifact feeds can be project- or organizational-scoped.

Project-Scoped Feeds

A project-scoped feed is scoped to a specified project, as opposed to an organization. The features of project-scoped feeds are as follows:

➤ **Visibility:** Project-scoped feeds inherit the visibility of the project they exist in. As a result, they can be visible to any identity that has access to the hosting project.

➤ **URL:** Since a project-scoped feed exists in the context of the project, the feed URL includes the project. An example of a project-scoped NuGet feed URL is shown here:

```
https://pkgs.dev.azure.com/<ORGANIZATION_NAME>/<PROJECT_NAME>/_
packaging/<FEED_NAME>/nuget/v3/index.json
```

➤ **Accessibility:** Since a project-scoped feed exists in the context of the project, it can be accessed and viewed only through the project hosting it.

Organization-Scoped Feeds

Like the name implies, an organization-scoped feed is scoped to an organization. The features are as follows:

➤ **Visibility:** Organization-scoped feeds inherit the visibility of the organization they exist in. As a result, they are private by default and visible only to the organization.

➤ **URL:** The URL of an organization-scoped feed does not include a project. Here is an example of an organization-scoped NuGet feed URL:

```
https://pkgs.dev.azure.com/<ORGANIZATION_NAME>/_packaging/<FEED_NAME>/
nuget/v3/index.json
```

➤ **Accessibility:** All organization-scoped feeds are accessed from the main feeds menu in Azure Artifacts since they are not tethered to any project.

How to Create an Azure Artifacts Feed

In this section, you will see how to create an artifact feed in Azure Artifacts. This feed is a tool that can allow you to store and manage your packages. To create an Azure Artifacts feed, follow these steps:

1. Log in to your Azure DevOps dashboard. After successfully logging in, you should see a page that looks similar to the one shown in Figure 7.1.

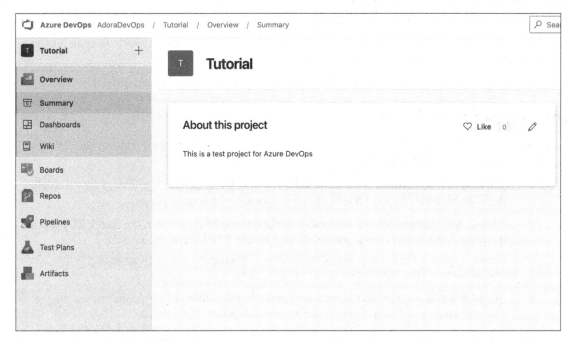

FIGURE 7.1: Azure DevOps dashboard

2. Select Artifacts in the left sidebar. After this, click the Create Feed button (Figure 7.2).

3. In the Create New Feed window, enter a name for your feed and set the visibility to Members of <your-organization>. Make sure you uncheck Upstream Sources, as we will cover that later in this chapter. You will be required to choose a scope. Select Project if you want to create a project-scoped feed or select Organization if you want to create an organization-scoped feed instead (Figure 7.3).

4. Click Create when you finish.

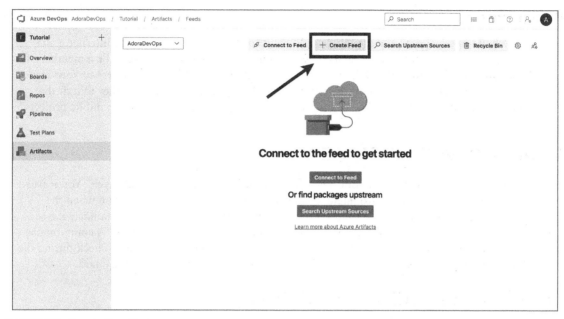

FIGURE 7.2: Create Feed button

FIGURE 7.3: Create New Feed window

Public Feeds

If you're building a project or library that you'd want to share publicly across the Internet, you should publish that project to a public feed. With public feeds, users don't have to be a member of your organization, and they also don't need an Azure DevOps account to gain access to your feed. One major characteristic of public feeds is that they are project-scoped feeds, so they inherit the visibility settings of the project. This means that public feeds can be created only in public projects.

AZURE ARTIFACTS FEED VIEWS

In previous sections, you learned about the different processes in the DevOps life cycle. You learned about deploying to a staging environment, testing, and then deploying to production when the application is stable. With Azure Artifacts feed views, you can achieve something similar with packages. Feed views enable developers to share specific package versions publicly. A common use case for feed views is to share stable package versions that pass the quality control check during the DevOps process, while holding back on packages that don't meet the quality benchmark.

Types of Azure Artifacts Feed Views

Azure Artifacts feeds have three views.

➤ `@local`

➤ `@prerelease`

➤ `@release`

The `@local` view is the default view that contains all the packages that are saved from upstream sources. The `@prerelease` and `@release` views are suggestions that can be edited or deleted.

> **A SUGGESTION FOR YOUR FEED VIEWS**
>
> The `@local` view contains all the versions of the package that are built, so this view gives you access to all deployment versions. When a feature in a library or package is ready to be tested, it can be promoted to the `@prerelease` view. In your team, you can choose to use this view to track versions that are currently being tested. Once the package is validated in different quality segments (e.g., code, security, and performance), then it can be promoted to the `@release` view. You can set a policy to allow your users to see packages only in the `@release` view so that you are confident your users will get features that have been quality checked.

UPSTREAM SOURCES

Let's imagine you're working on a project with multiple dependencies. In your project, there are some packages you create and use, but you also use some public packages from other sources. With upstream sources, you can use a single feed to curate and store packages from different sources. Once you create an upstream source, any user who has connected to your artifact feed can install a package from the original source (the upstream source), and a copy will be saved to the artifact feed. Subsequently, the copied version of the package in the artifact feed will become the copy that will be downloaded.

When dealing with large projects that have multiple dependencies, there are many advantages that upstream sources give, and some of them are listed here:

➤ **Simplicity:** All your configuration files reference only one feed, so it's easy to manage and there are less errors. For example, if you have multiple projects that share dependencies and you want to add a new source for dependencies, you update configuration files across multiple projects. However, if you use an upstream source, you add the new source in your artifact feed, and there is no need for other updates.

➤ **Security:** Forcing team projects to use upstream sources and controlling the permissions for who has access to managing upstream sources help teams contain the quality of package sources that their projects can use.

➤ **Availability:** When you install a package from an upstream source, a copy is also saved to your artifact feed. So if the upstream source is disabled or removed, you can continue to build your application because you'll have a copy of that package in your artifact feed.

Setting Up Upstream Sources

When building applications, software development teams use different dependencies in the project. As you now know, using upstream sources can help you manage these dependencies in one central location. This section will cover the following:

➤ How to update a feed to use an upstream source

➤ How to create a feed with upstream source capability

➤ How to add a feed in your organization to an upstream source

How to Update a Feed to Use an Upstream Source

In a previous section, you created an Azure Artifacts feed without enabling upstream sources. To enable upstream sources for the feed you created, go back to it and follow these steps:

1. Click the gear button to navigate to the Feeds settings (Figure 7.4).

2. Select the Upstream Sources tab and click Add Upstream (Figure 7.5).

3. In the Add Upstream Source window, select Public Source, and choose a source (Figure 7.6). Figure 7.7 shows Npmjs as the chosen public source, but you can choose a source you need in your project.

4. Click Save when you finish, and you should see the new upstream source in your list of upstream sources (Figure 7.8).

FIGURE 7.4: Navigating to the feed settings

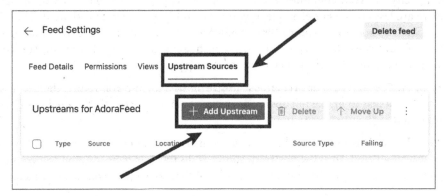

FIGURE 7.5: Feed Settings window

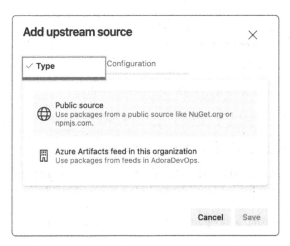

FIGURE 7.6: Adding an upstream source

You have now successfully added an upstream source to an existing artifact feed. This means you can connect to this feed in your project, as opposed to the upstream source directly, and through this feed, you can get all the packages that are published to the upstream source. For example, Express is a popular Node framework used for building back-end applications. By connecting to AdoraFeed (the artifact feed shown in this section), I can download Express because I have Npmjs as an upstream source.

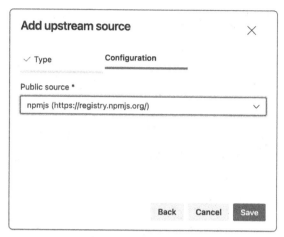

FIGURE 7.7: Choosing an upstream source

FIGURE 7.8: List of upstream sources

How to Create a Feed with Upstream Source Capability

In this section, we will create another Azure Artifact feed and enable upstream sources. To learn how to do this, follow these steps:

1. Go to the Artifacts dashboard and click Create Feed.

2. In the Create New Feed window, enter a name for your feed and set the visibility to Members of <your-organization>. Select Upstream Sources so that your new feed will have different upstream sources. You will be required to choose a scope. Select Project if you want to create a project-scoped feed or select Organization if you want to create an organization-scoped feed instead (Figure 7.9).

3. Click Create when you finish.

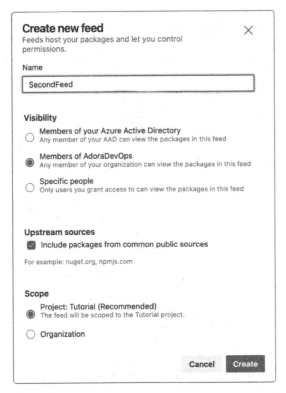

FIGURE 7.9: Creating a feed with upstream sources

You have now created a feed that has multiple upstream sources. To view the list of upstream sources available in this feed, follow these steps:

1.   In the feed, click the gear button. This will take you to the Feed settings (Figure 7.10).

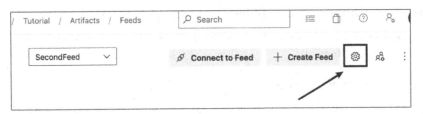

FIGURE 7.10: Navigating to the Feed settings

2.   Select the Upstream Sources tab. Here, you will see a list of upstream sources available to your feed (Figure 7.11).

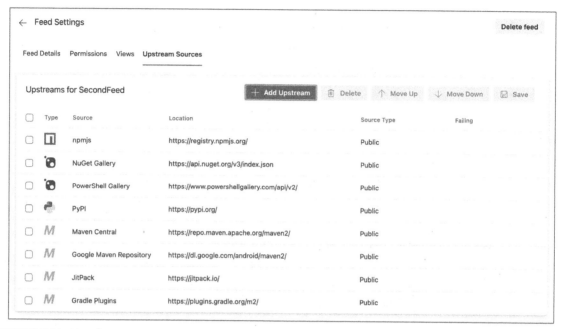

FIGURE 7.11: List of upstream sources

These are all the default upstream sources offered by Azure. You can add other custom upstream sources to your feed, and that is what we will cover in the next section.

How to Add a Feed in Your Organization to an Upstream Source

So far, we have been adding popular registries such as Npmjs and NuGet as upstream sources, but you can also add an artifact feed. Since an artifact feed copies packages from different upstream sources, it can also be an upstream source for other feeds to copy packages from. To add an Azure Artifacts feed in your organization as an upstream source, follow these steps:

1. Go to the Artifact dashboard, and click the gear button to navigate to the Feed settings.

2. Select Upstream Sources and click Add Upstream.

3. In the Add Upstream Source window, click Azure Artifacts Feed In This Organization (Figure 7.12).

4. Now it's time to configure your upstream source. Select the feed you want to add, choose the view and the package types you want this source to use, and name your upstream source. Click Save when you're done. In Figure 7.13, I am using my feed called SecondFeed and adding only the NuGet and npm package types.

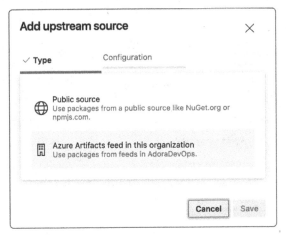

FIGURE 7.12: Adding an Azure Artifacts feed as an upstream source

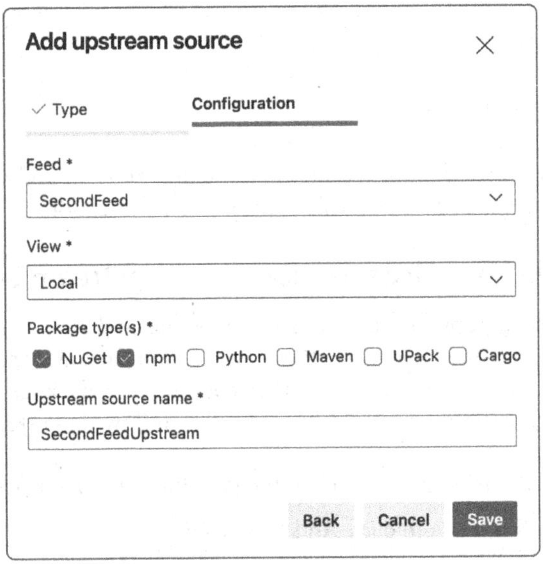

Add upstream source ✕

✓ **Type**   **Configuration**

Feed *

SecondFeed ⌄

View *

Local ⌄

Package type(s) *

☑ NuGet ☑ npm ☐ Python ☐ Maven ☐ UPack ☐ Cargo

Upstream source name *

SecondFeedUpstream

Back   Cancel   **Save**

FIGURE 7.13: Configuring the upstream source

You have successfully added a feed in your organization as an upstream source in another feed. Figure 7.14 shows what that looks like for me; you should have something similar. Since I chose only NuGet and npm as package types, those are the only upstream sources from the feed that get imported.

FIGURE 7.14: Upstream sources from existing feed

PUBLISHING ARTIFACTS IN AZURE PIPELINES

During the build stage in your CI/CD pipeline, you will probably need to publish pipeline artifacts so that you can use the files at a later stage in your pipeline. In this section, you will see how to publish your artifacts using YAML and the classic editor.

Publishing Artifacts Using the publish Keyword in YAML

If you already have a YAML file for your build, you can add this step in your file to publish a specific path as an artifact.

```
Steps:
- publish: $(System.DefaultWorkingDirectory)/website/dist
    artifact: website
```

In the previous code snippet, Azure Pipelines would publish the /website/dist directory and its content as an artifact. The name of the artifact is website. Naming an artifact creates a unique identifier for the artifact so that you can reference it later when you want to download it. To publish contents of a specific file path, you can replace /website/dist with the specific file path for your file contents.

Publishing Artifacts Using a YAML Task

Azure Pipelines also has a pipeline task that you can use to publish artifacts. To use this task instead, see the following code snippet:

```
steps:
- task: PublishPipelineArtifact@1
    inputs:
      targetPath: $(System.DefaultWorkingDirectory)/website/dist
      artifactName: website
```

`targetPath` is the path to the folder or file you'd like to publish, while `artifactName` is the name of the artifact you want to create. When using this YAML task, you should update these two fields with the appropriate values for your project.

Publishing Artifacts Using the Classic Editor

You can also publish pipeline artifacts from the classic editor by adding a pipeline task. To do this, follow these steps:

1. Navigate to the pipeline dashboard and choose the build pipeline for which you'd like to publish artifacts. Note that this has to be a classic editor pipeline (Figure 7.15).

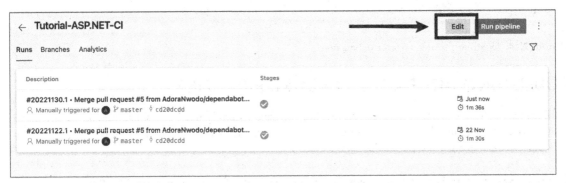

FIGURE 7.15: Build pipeline

2. In the pipeline, click Edit. That will bring you to the classic editor (Figure 7.16).

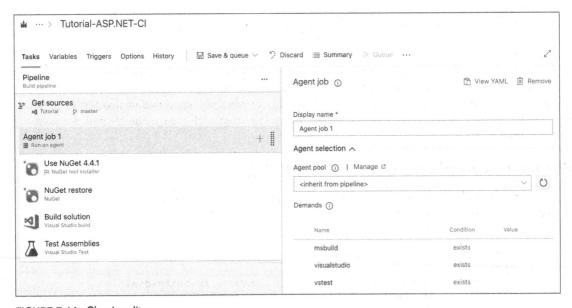

FIGURE 7.16: Classic editor

3. Here, you can see a list of jobs that your pipeline executes (your jobs might be different from mine depending on your project). Since this is an ASP.NET project, we will pack the project first. This creates a NuGet package that can be published. To pack the project, add a NuGet task to the pipeline (Figure 7.17).

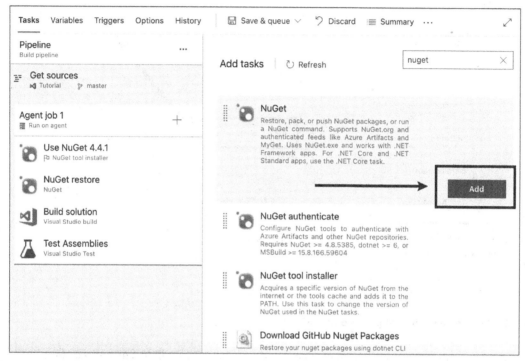

FIGURE 7.17: Adding a NuGet task to a pipeline

4. NuGet has different commands. To run the `pack` command, select Pack in the command drop-down list (Figure 7.18).

   As shown in Figure 7.18, you should edit other fields as you deem fit. However, some settings should look like this:

   Display name: NuGet Pack
   Command: pack
   Path to csproj or nuspec file(s) to pack: **/*.csproj

5. Now it's time to publish the artifact that you packed in the previous step. NuGet also has a task for that, so let's go ahead and use it (Figure 7.19). Add another NuGet task to the pipeline (right below the NuGet pack task) and edit some settings to look like this:

   Display name: NuGet Push
   Command: push
   NuGet package(s) to publish: $(Build.ArtifactStagingDirectory)/**/*.
   nupkg;!$(Build.ArtifactStagingDirectory)/**/*.symbols.nupkg
   Target feed location: This organization/collection
   Target feed: AdoraFeed (the name of your feed)

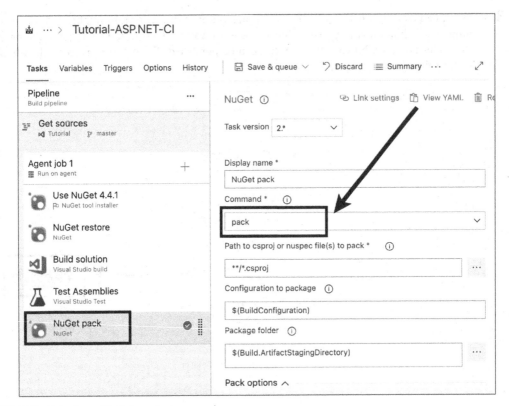

FIGURE 7.18: Creating a NuGet pack command

6. In the top menu, click Save & Queue and wait for your build to finish successfully.

   You can also publish pipeline artifacts from the classic editor by adding a Publish Pipeline Artifacts task. This can be useful when you are not working on ASP.NET projects or projects that use NuGet. To do this, follow these steps:

1. Depending on the project, you will need to build the project and create an artifact from that build.

2. Add the Publish Pipeline Artifact task, and fill out the following fields:

   Display name: Publish artifact (or any name you like)
   File or directory path: $(Build.ArtifactStagingDirectory)/build/ (the path to publish)

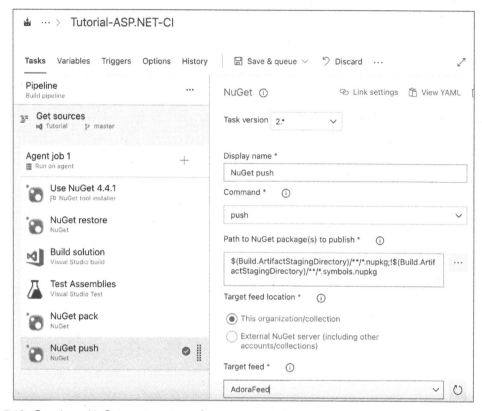

FIGURE 7.19: Creating a NuGet push command

Artifact name: website (name of the artifact, different from display name of the build step)
Artifact publish location: Choose whether to store the artifact in Azure Pipelines, or to copy it to a file share that must be accessible from the pipeline agent

Your classic editor should look like Figure 7.20.

3. In the top menu, click Save & Queue and wait for your build to finish successfully.

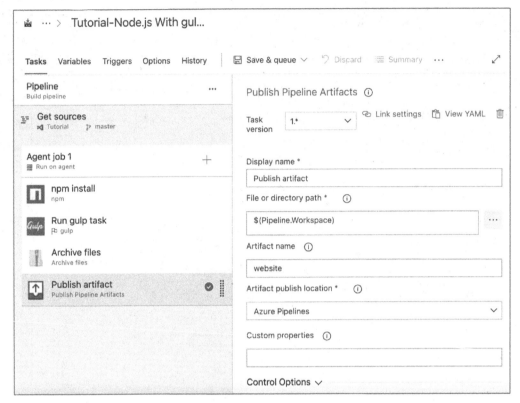

FIGURE 7.20: Creating a Publish Pipeline Artifacts task

DOWNLOADING ARTIFACTS IN AZURE PIPELINES

In your pipeline, you can also download artifacts that you published in a different stage. These artifacts can be used for deployments, testing, or other actions you might want to perform. In this section, you will see how to publish your artifacts using YAML and the classic editor.

Downloading Artifacts Using the Download Keyword in YAML

If you already have a YAML file for your build, you can add this step in your file to download a specific path as an artifact.

In the following code snippet, Azure Pipelines will download the website in the current pipeline. Files are downloaded to `$(Pipeline.Workspace)` by default. If no artifact name is specified, a subfolder is created for each downloaded artifact.

```
steps:
- download: current
  artifact: website
```

Downloading Artifacts Using a YAML Task

Azure Pipelines also has a pipeline task that you can use to download artifacts. To use this task instead, see the following code snippet:

```
steps:
- task: DownloadPipelineArtifact@2
  inputs:
    artifact: website
```

`DownloadPipelineArtifact@2` is the name of the task and should not be edited. However, the artifact field can be edited (or ignored). If the `artifact` field is specified, then it will download just that artifact. However, if it's not specified, then all artifacts associated with the pipeline will be downloaded.

Downloading Artifacts Using the Classic Editor

You can also publish pipeline artifacts from the classic editor by adding a pipeline task. To do this, follow these steps:

1. Navigate to the pipeline dashboard and choose the build pipeline that you'd like to publish artifacts for. Note that this has to be a classic editor pipeline.

2. In the pipeline, click Edit. That will bring you to the classic editor.

3. Add the Download Pipeline Artifact task to your pipeline and fill out the following fields:

    Display name: Download artifact (or any name you like)
    Download artifacts produced by: download artifacts produced by the current pipeline run or from a specific pipeline run
    Artifact name: website (name of the artifact to download)
    Matching patterns: File matching patterns to control which files get downloaded
    Destination directory: directory to download the artifact files to

    Your classic editor should look like Figure 7.21.

4. In the top menu, click Save & Queue and wait for your build to finish successfully.

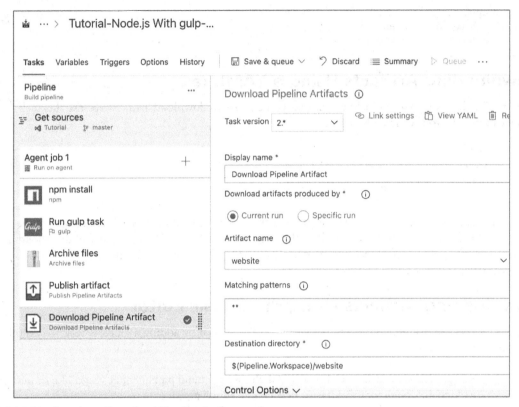

FIGURE 7.21: Creating a Download Pipeline Artifacts task

SUMMARY

An artifact is a deployable component of your application. The primary purpose of an artifact repository is to securely store artifacts that are created during the software development process.

Artifact repositories store two kinds of artifacts: build artifacts and deployment artifacts. Build artifacts are the outputs of the continuous integration step in your pipeline. Deployment artifacts are executables that are released for the public to use. They are generated during the deployment stage of the pipeline.

Azure Artifacts supports several types of packages, including NuGet, npm, Python, Maven, and universal packages. Build artifacts and symbols are also supported within Azure Artifacts.

An Azure Artifacts feed is a cloud-based location where you can keep and organize software packages. Artifact feeds are not unique to the type of package. Azure Artifact feeds can be project- or organizational-scoped. A project-scoped feed is scoped to a specified project, as opposed to an organization. An organization-scoped feed is scoped to an organization.

With upstream sources, you can use a single feed to curate and store packages from different sources. Once you create an upstream source, any user who has connected to your artifact feed can install a package from the original source (the upstream source) and a copy will be saved to the artifact feed.

In Azure Pipelines, you can publish and download artifacts using YAML, YAML tasks, and the classic editor.

Chapter 8 is a deep dive into code deployments, release pipelines, and how to automate release pipelines using Azure Pipelines.

8

Automating Code Deployments with Azure Pipelines

This chapter goes deeper into discussing the continuous deployment and continuous delivery processes in the DevOps life cycle. You will also learn about release pipelines, and you will see how to use this feature to automate your code deployments.

What You Will Learn in This Chapter

➤ Continuous Deployment and Continuous Delivery in DevOps

➤ Continuous Deployment

➤ Continuous Delivery

➤ Release Pipelines

➤ Advantages of Release Pipelines

➤ How Release Pipelines Work in Azure

➤ Deployment Model Using Azure Release Pipelines

➤ Creating the Release Pipeline

➤ Creating a Release

➤ Multistage Pipelines

➤ Summary

CONTINUOUS DEPLOYMENT AND CONTINUOUS DELIVERY IN DevOps

Previous chapters covered continuous integration in depth, and you now know that continuous integration involves merging, testing, and building code. The output of continuous integration, which is usually the packaged code, is the input for continuous deployment or continuous delivery. Chapter 5 also defined and introduced continuous deployment and continuous delivery to you, and in this section, you will learn more about these two concepts.

Continuous Deployment

In the continuous deployment methodology, code updates to an application are automatically released into the production environment. A set of predetermined tests serves as the engine for this automation. The automation tools push updates to the production environments immediately after they pass those tests.

With continuous deployments, software changes can make their way to production without manual testing and manual approvals. Although this means that software development teams can ship features faster, checking in unstable code that somehow makes its way past automated tests can make production environments unstable quickly. To create a successful continuous deployment strategy across the board, you should begin with making your continuous integration workflow seamless and then streamline and automate the application release and rollback process so you can release new releases frequently and roll back if the need ever arises. Software development teams must implement real-time monitoring for the production environment to swiftly recognize and manage any technical issues that occur after a new deployment because continuous deployment also introduces a risk to the software release process.

THE IMPORTANCE OF AUTOMATION

For teams using continuous deployment, automation is important for productivity. To ensure that new code commits are functional before they are deployed, a strong set of automated tests must be programmed and should run in the pipeline. When the tests fail or show that the software update is of low quality, tools are needed to halt the deployment process and initiate human intervention. It is also through automation that the code is deployed.

Continuous Deployment Tools

Software developers must leverage the right tools for establishing efficient DevOps practices to continuously develop and deploy high-quality software updates. By doing this, errors in the pipeline for delivering software are reduced or removed while also ensuring effective communication across the board. The following are some of the important tools that should exist in the continuous deployment workflow:

➤ **Secrets management tools:** During deployments, the virtual machine running the scripts may need access to secrets or passwords, and it is not ideal to store these in plain text anywhere in the pipeline scripts. Integrating a secrets management tool with your continuous deployment workflow enables the pipeline to read secrets and passwords without any security risk.

➤ **Configuration management tools:** The consistency of all the software and application infrastructure is maintained by configuration management tools.

➤ **Rollback tools:** When a software update that is not of good quality is made, a quick rollback prevents the application from staying in a bad state for a long time. This means that rollback tools (or rollback scripts) are important in continuous deployment.

➤ **Release automation tools:** When automating all the tasks required to support continuous deployment, application release automation tools are necessary. These tools are used with the configuration management tools to guarantee that all deployment environments are suitably provisioned and capable of operating at their peak efficiency.

➤ **Infrastructure and application monitoring tools:** After deployment, it's critical to have access to data on the application and infrastructure's performance. Infrastructure and application monitoring tools assist in determining whether the updates made had a favorable or unfavorable effect on the entire application.

Advantages of Continuous Deployment

This section highlights some of the benefits of continuous deployment in software engineering teams.

➤ **Faster releases:** There is no need to pause development for releases so software development teams can create software more quickly. For every change, deployment pipelines are automatically triggered.

➤ **Smaller releases:** At every point, small batches of changes get deployed. This means that releases are smaller and easier to fix if an issue arises.

➤ **Reduces (or eliminates) manual intervention:** The use of automation in the process of deploying applications is what distinguishes continuous deployment. Especially with regard to release testing, continuous deployment encourages developers to fully automate the software development life cycle. Automation does more than just hasten the release of new releases for developers. Furthermore, it cuts down on the time needed for manual tasks.

➤ **Faster customer feedback:** The customer feedback loop will be faster if your application is updated more often. Software development teams can evaluate the effects of a new change on user engagement or behavior and make adjustments as necessary by utilizing cutting-edge monitoring tools. When customer behavior indicates that a quick pivot or change in strategy is required, the capacity to release changes quickly is a benefit.

Continuous Delivery

In continuous delivery, the application builds are automatically deployed into an environment for automatic quality assurance testing, which checks for a variety of errors and inconsistencies. Continuous delivery mandates human intervention to approve deployments into production after the code passes all tests. The deployment is then carried out automatically. This is unlike a continuous deployment model, where deployments go from development to production automatically and without human intervention. The three foundations of continuous delivery are configuration management, continuous integration, and continuous testing.

Advantages of Continuous Delivery

This section highlights some of the benefits of continuous delivery in software engineering teams.

➤ **Faster releases:** The traditional phased software delivery life cycle's integration and test/fix phase frequently lasts weeks or even months. Regression testing and integration can be entirely eliminated from the development process when teams collaborate to automate the build and deployment, environment provisioning, and testing procedures. The extensive amounts of rework in the traditional approach are also avoided.

➤ **Low-risk deployments:** Software deployments should be easy, low-risk processes that can be carried out whenever needed. This is the main objective of continuous delivery. It is relatively easy to achieve zero-downtime deployments by implementing continuous delivery patterns like blue-green deployments.

WHAT ARE BLUE-GREEN DEPLOYMENTS?

A blue-green deployment is a method of delivering software in which you make two different but related environments. The new application version is running in the green environment, while the current application version is running in the blue environment. By making the rollback procedure simpler in the event that a deployment fails, using a blue-green deployment strategy increases application availability and lowers deployment risk. The blue environment is deprecated, and the live application traffic is switched to the green environment once testing on the green environment is finished.

➤ **Quality products:** Since application updates are rigorously tested and validated in a quality assurance environment before software release to production, customers are guaranteed better-quality products with fewer to no bugs.

RELEASE PIPELINES

An organization's software release pipeline encapsulates all the manual and automated steps necessary to guarantee that customers can access a dependable, secure version of the product. It covers everything concerning software validation and releases with a focus on getting changes into end users' hands. The practice of making sure your codebase is prepared to deploy safely at any time, known as *continuous delivery* (or *continuous deployment*), goes hand in hand with it.

Depending on your software release model (continuous delivery or continuous deployment), your release pipeline can be triggered manually or automatically due to other events in your CI/CD pipeline. Since release pipelines deploy already built application artifacts, they need to be connected to the artifact repository so that they can retrieve the needed artifacts to be deployed.

Advantages of Release Pipelines

Release pipelines are valuable in software development teams for these reasons:

➤ Release pipelines shorten the wait for a new release while maintaining stability. As a result, your users will have quicker access to new features (or bug fixes), and you'll have fail-safes and automatic rollback processes in place just in case.

➤ Release pipelines also aid in boosting developer productivity. Software developers do not have to waste time re-creating builds after the fact because the pipeline automates tedious tasks. They can concentrate more on writing the code itself, which is actually the work that adds value to the organization.

➤ Since software developers are not focused on mundane tasks involved in software releases and rollbacks, engineering effort isn't spent on time-consuming things, and this can reduce costs for the team in the long run.

Software developers are also customers for some products. As customers and software users, a lot of us have experienced downtime either on social media or in some utility tools we use. However, for many products the downtime doesn't last as long. This is because the teams have built an efficient DevOps process, and this is reflected in their code releases as well as in rollbacks. If these processes were not efficient, we would have bad experiences as customers.

How Release Pipelines Work in Azure

Previous sections covered the fundamentals and benefits of release pipelines. In this section, you will learn about how release pipelines work in Azure, which will prepare you for creating your own release pipeline.

As part of every software release, Azure Pipelines runs the following steps:

1. **Predeployment approval:** First, Azure Pipelines determines whether a predeployment approval is necessary before deploying a release to a stage when a new deployment request is triggered.

2. **Queue deployment job:** Once the predeployment checks pass, Azure Pipelines schedules the deployment job on an available deployment agent in the specified agent pool (agents and agent pools were covered in Chapter 5).

3. **Agent selection:** In this step, the deployment job is picked up by the deployment agent.

4. **Download artifacts:** The deployment agent downloads all the artifacts that the release requires.

5. **Execute deployment:** At this point, all predeployment processes have been completed, and the deployment agent will run all the tasks associated with the deployment job.

6. **Logging:** For each stage of the deployment process, the agent generates thorough logs and pushes them back to Azure Pipelines.

7. **Postdeployment approval:** When deployment to a stage is complete, Azure Pipelines checks to see whether a postdeployment approval is necessary for that stage. It moves on to initiate deployment to the next stage if no approval is mandated or after completing a required approval (Figure 8.1).

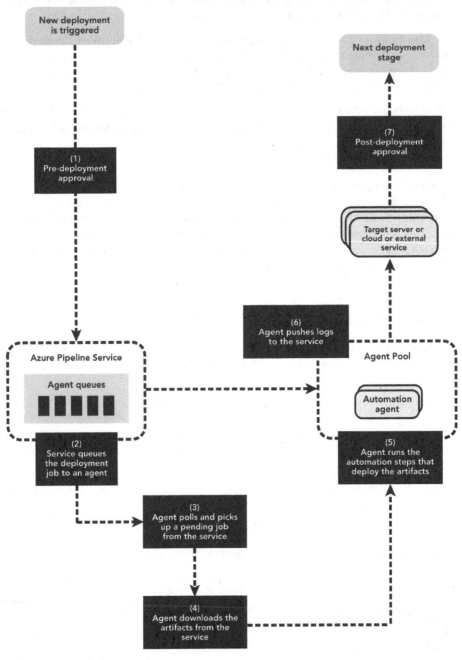

FIGURE 8.1: How release pipelines work

Deployment Model Using Azure Release Pipelines

Like the build pipeline, a release consists of at least one stage, and each stage consists of different jobs and tasks. Figure 8.2 shows a deployment model using Azure release pipelines.

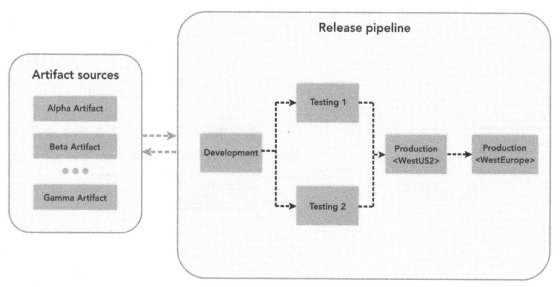

FIGURE 8.2: Deployment models using Azure release pipelines

In Figure 8.2, the pipeline is composed of three build artifacts from three different build pipelines. The artifacts are called Alpha Artifact, Beta Artifact, and Gamma Artifact. The application is first deployed to the Development stage and then forked to two Testing stages. If deployment succeeds in both Testing stages, the application will be deployed to Production WestUS2 and then to Production WestEurope. Each production deployment represents multiple instances of the same application deployed to various geographical locations.

Creating the Release Pipeline

To create a release pipeline in Azure DevOps, follow the steps described here:

1. Navigate to the Pipelines dashboard and select Releases from the left menu. Click the New Pipeline button (Figure 8.3).

2. After you create the pipeline, you will see a list of templates for release pipelines. You can deploy different types of applications to Azure App Service, Kubernetes Clusters, Azure Functions, and more. However, for this example, you will be creating a release pipeline for an App Service deployment, so select Azure App Service Deployment and click Apply (Figure 8.4).

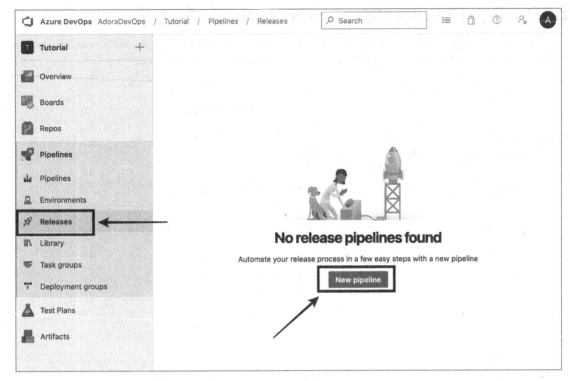

FIGURE 8.3: Creating a new release pipeline

FIGURE 8.4: Selecting a release pipeline template

3.   Next, provide a stage name. This will be the identifier for the stage that will contain the deployment jobs and tasks. In Figure 8.5, the stage is called Deploy Website.

4. In the Stages section, click 1 job, 1 task. There you will be able to supply the details of the Azure app service resource you want your website to be deployed to (Figure 8.6).

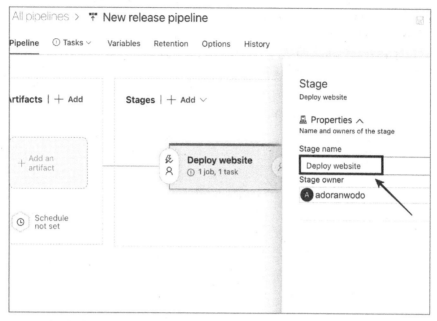

FIGURE 8.5: Naming the deployment stage

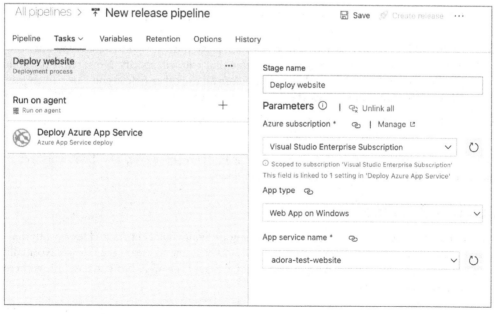

FIGURE 8.6: Adding stage properties

At this point, you have already added all the information required to create a single-stage release pipeline. However, this pipeline cannot work yet because there is no artifact connected to it, so the pipeline has no packaged code to release to Azure App Service. The next steps in this section will involve importing the artifact repository into your work-in-progress release pipeline.

5. Go back to the Pipeline tab to access the New Release Pipeline home screen. Click Add An Artifact to start your import (Figure 8.7).

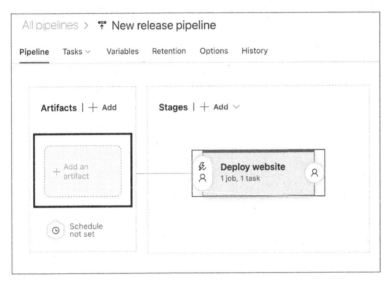

FIGURE 8.7: Connecting an artifact to the release pipeline

6. In the Add An Artifact window that pops up, leave Build as your source type since the artifact will be created from a build pipeline that you will specify. Now, select the build pipeline you want to use for this and populate all the other fields (you can also choose to leave them as they are). Click the Add button when you are done (Figure 8.8).

7. At the top-right corner, click the Save button to save the release pipeline settings that you just created (Figure 8.9).

You have now successfully created a release pipeline in Azure. However, it will not work yet until you create a release; the next section will cover that in detail.

Creating a Release

A release represents continuous delivery (or continuous deployment) in Azure DevOps. In the previous section, you set up a release pipeline, and now it's time to create the release. Normally, a release is automatically triggered when a new build artifact is created, but you can follow these steps to manually step up your release:

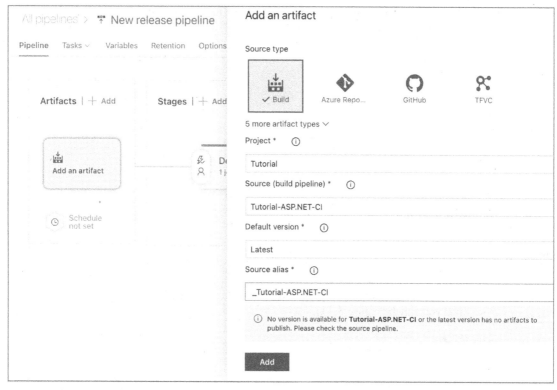

FIGURE 8.8: Specifying artifact properties

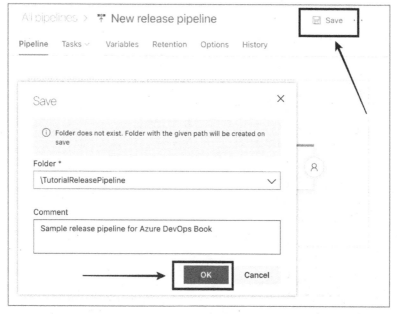

FIGURE 8.9: Saving the release pipeline

1. On the home page of the release pipeline you created in the previous section, click Create Release in the top-right corner (Figure 8.10).

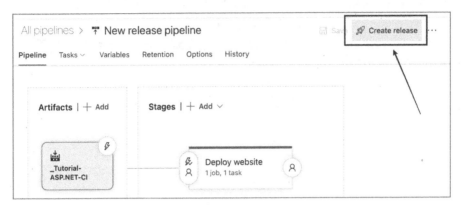

FIGURE 8.10: Creating a release

2. Enter a description for your release and check that the right artifacts are selected. Click Create once you finish (Figure 8.11).

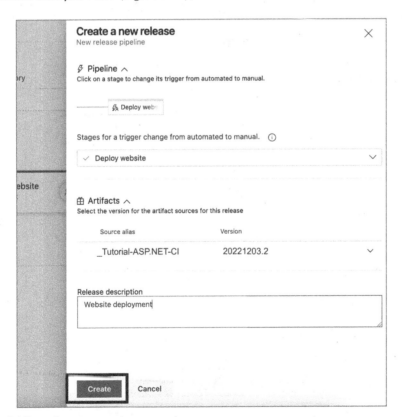

FIGURE 8.11: Adding release properties

3. After saving, a banner would appear at the top of the page, and this indicates that the release has been created successfully (Figure 8.12).

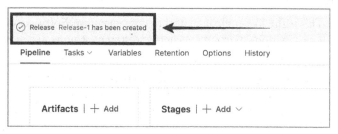

FIGURE 8.12: Release created successfully

4. You can now click the release and see details about the run (Figure 8.13).

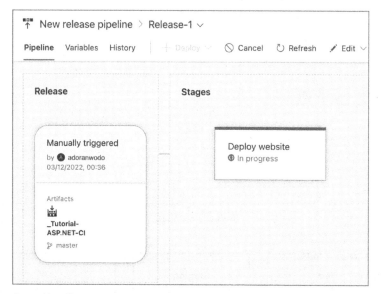

FIGURE 8.13: New release details

MULTISTAGE PIPELINES

When working on live applications that customers use, you will hardly ever deploy to one environment like you did in the previous section. More often than not, you will use multistage pipelines. A common approach for many software engineering teams when creating deployments is to have multiple environments. The environments might look similar to the environments described here:

➤ **Test:** This environment enables QA engineers to test new and modified code using automated or manual methodologies.

➤ **Staging:** The goal of this environment, which is essentially a replica of the production environment, is to ensure that the software operates properly by closely simulating a real production environment. With this environment, testing at a level close to production can be done in a nonproduction setting to ensure that the application will perform as intended after deployment.

➤ **Production:** This is the live environment that customers use. Software development teams can have multiple production environments across different regions depending on the requirements of their application.

A multistage release pipeline is used to deploy to these environments one after the other in multiple stages. Figure 8.14 illustrates how multistage pipelines work. First, when the release pipeline is triggered, the application gets deployed to the test environment. If that deployment is successful, then a deployment to the staging environment is triggered next. If all goes well in staging, then the application will also be deployed to production. However, if a deployment fails, the logs show the failure, and the pipeline terminates. After getting the failure notification, the software development teams can work on fixing the failing release pipeline deployment (Figure 8.14).

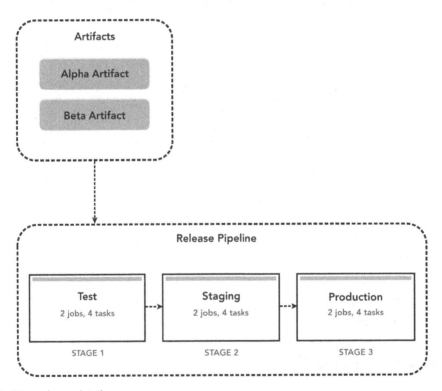

FIGURE 8.14: New release details

The following steps show how to create a multistage release pipeline in Azure Pipelines:

1. Navigate to the Pipelines dashboard and select Releases from the left menu. Click the New Pipeline button.

2. Create and save a release pipeline for an App Service deployment like you did in the previous section (Figure 8.15).

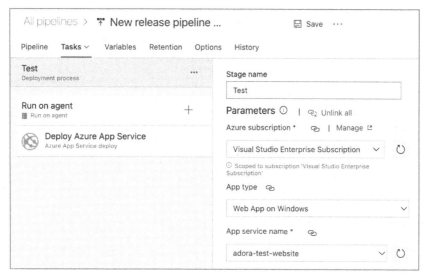

FIGURE 8.15: Creating the first stage

3. After creating the first stage, click the Add button and select New Stage to create your second stage (see Figure 8.16). As usual, set it to Azure App Service deployment, name the stage (see Figure 8.17), and set the properties (see Figure 8.18). This stage will deploy the staging resources, so your stage name will be Staging.

FIGURE 8.16: Adding a new stage to the pipeline

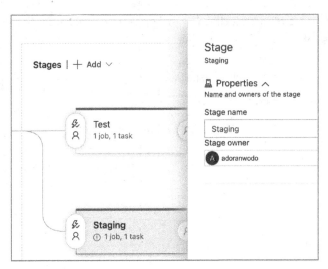

FIGURE 8.17: Renaming the second stage

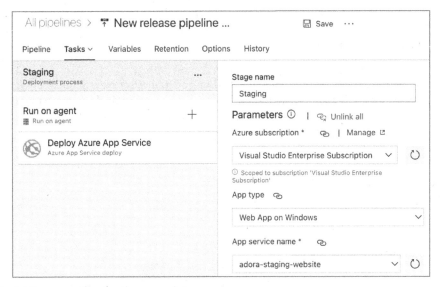

FIGURE 8.18: Adding properties for the second stage

4. If you added a new stage (as opposed to cloning an existing stage), your new stage (staging) will not depend on your previous stage (test). They will look similar to Figure 8.19.

You will add the dependency manually. To do so, click Pre-Deployment Conditions For Staging (Figure 8.20).

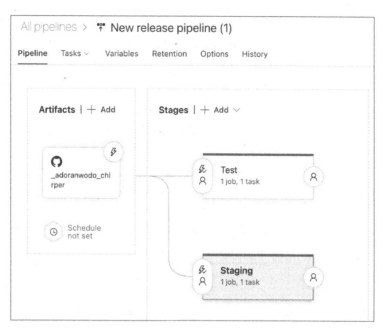

FIGURE 8.19: Adding properties for the second stage

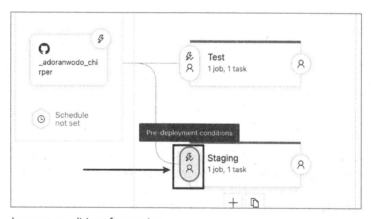

FIGURE 8.20: Predeployment conditions for staging

Here, you can set a bunch of conditions that should be satisfied before the Staging stage runs. The first condition you want to set is that Staging should run only after Test has run successfully.

To do this, set the trigger to After Stage and select the Test stage. What this means is that the Staging stage will get triggered only after the Test stage has run completely (Figure 8.21).

Now, you can see that Staging depends on Test, as it should (Figure 8.22).

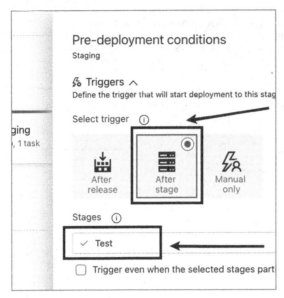

FIGURE 8.21: Setting deployment triggers

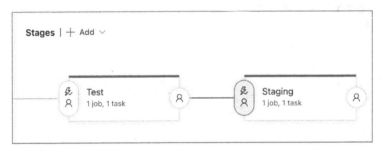

FIGURE 8.22: Staging now depends on Test

5. You can also add more conditions if you like. Here, I will show how to add approvals to your pipeline stages. This is particularly useful if you want to restrict approvals of deployments to certain environments (e.g., the engineering manager wants to deploy to production only after the QA team has validated that the staging environment is stable and the application is ready to ship). To add approvals, enable predeployment approvals and add the identities of the users who should have approve privilege. Figure 8.23 illustrates how to do this.

6. You have successfully added approvals, so the next time your release pipeline runs, a deployment to Staging will not happen without an approval from the specified user.

7. To create the final stage (Production), repeat the steps used in creating stage 2. After that, your pipeline should look like the one in Figure 8.24.

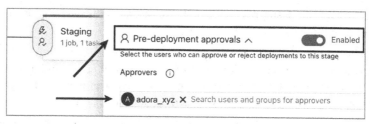

FIGURE 8.23: Predeployment approvals

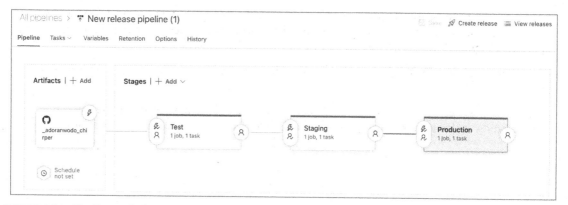

FIGURE 8.24: Pipeline with three stages

You have successfully created a multistage release pipeline with three stages and approvals for the next stage. Like the single-stage release pipeline, you can create a release to trigger this and watch your deployment go all the way to the end.

PRACTICE WORK

Most of the tutorials in this chapter will help you get started creating release pipelines. However, there are some things you can practice to cement your knowledge.

On your own, try creating a multistage pipeline with different kinds of predeployment conditions as well as postdeployment conditions. Add approvals, triggers, and other kinds of conditions (settings) that you come across. Practicing these concepts is how you get better at using Azure Pipelines and the entire Azure DevOps suite.

SUMMARY

With continuous deployments, software changes can make their way to production without manual testing and manual approvals.

Some continuous deployment tools include secrets management tools, configuration management tools, rollback tools, release automation tools, and monitoring tools.

Continuous deployments aid faster releases, smaller releases, and a faster customer feedback loop. It also reduces human intervention in software deployments.

In continuous delivery, the application builds are automatically deployed into an environment for automatic quality assurance testing, which checks for a variety of errors and inconsistencies. Continuous delivery mandates human intervention to approve deployments into production after the code passes all tests. The deployment is then carried out automatically.

An organization's software release pipeline encapsulates all the manual and automated steps necessary to guarantee that customers can access a dependable, secure version of the product.

As part of every software release, Azure Pipelines runs the following steps: predeployment approval, queue deployment job, agent selection, download artifacts, execute deployment, logging, and postdeployment approval.

A multistage release pipeline is used to deploy to these environments one after the other in multiple stages.

Chapter 9 is a deep dive into Azure Test Plans. There, you will learn more about test plans and test suites. You will also learn how to run manual and automated tests using Azure Test Plans.

Application Testing with Azure Test Plans

This chapter covers Azure Test Plans and how you can use this tool to run manual and automated tests for your application.

What You Will Learn in This Chapter

- ➤ Overview of Azure Test Plans
  - ➤ How Azure Test Plans Work
  - ➤ Advantages of Azure Test Plans
- ➤ Creating Test Plans and Test Suites
  - ➤ Test Plans
  - ➤ Test Suites
- ➤ Test Cases
  - ➤ Overview of Test Cases
  - ➤ Creating Test Cases
- ➤ Configurations in Tests
  - ➤ Creating Test Configurations
  - ➤ Assigning Test Configurations
- ➤ Running Manual Tests
  - ➤ Running Tests with Configurations
  - ➤ Viewing Manual Test Results

➤ Running Automated Tests from Test Plans

   ➤ Setting Up Your Environment for Automated Tests

   ➤ Running the Tests

➤ Summary

OVERVIEW OF AZURE TEST PLANS

With Azure Test Plans, quality assurance teams can utilize the powerful tools provided to promote quality and teamwork throughout the development process. Azure Test Plans is a simple-to-use test management tool that offers all the mechanisms necessary for running different application tests. With Azure Test Plans, you can perform user acceptance testing, exploratory testing, and planned manual testing. You can also use the tool to get feedback from important stakeholders.

How Azure Test Plans Work

Azure Test Plans supports different types of testing goals by combining different testing tools, progress reports, and more. This section will cover some of the testing goals that Azure Test Plans supports.

➤ **Manual testing:** Azure Test Plans can be used to plan manual testing by organizing these tests into test plans and test suites. This kind of testing involves validating the application against its requirements without using any automated testing tools.

➤ **Exploratory testing:** The software testing methodology known as *exploratory testing* is frequently referred to as learning, test design, and execution occurring concurrently. It emphasizes discovery and depends on the direction of the individual tester to find flaws that are difficult to cover when running other application tests. Azure Test Plans supports exploratory testing with the Test and Feedback extension.

WHEN IS EXPLORATORY TESTING IDEAL?

Exploratory testing is best used in particular testing situations, such as when someone needs to quickly learn about a product and give prompt feedback. It aids in evaluating a product's quality from the viewpoint of the customer.

Exploratory testing also makes sure you don't overlook edge cases that cause crucial quality failures when testing applications with special features. Additionally, you can use exploratory testing to support the unit test process, document the steps, and use that knowledge to extensively test the application going forward.

➤ **User acceptance testing:** User acceptance testing (UAT) is a type of testing carried out by the client or end user to confirm or accept the application features before moving the application to the production environment. It makes sure teams provide the value customers have requested. You can make UAT test plans and suites, invite numerous testers to run these tests, and use simple charts to track the progress and outcomes of the tests.

➤ **Automated testing:** Running tests within Azure Pipelines facilitates automated testing. Analyzing your test data for builds and releases is made possible by test analytics. It increases pipeline efficiency by locating recurrent, significant quality problems. Azure Test Plans supports automated testing by doing the following:

➤ Connecting build or release pipelines with test plans or test cases

➤ Providing prebuilt reports and programmable dashboard widgets to show pipeline testing results

➤ Using the analytics system aggregate test results and associated test data

➤ **Stakeholder feedback:** To create high-quality software that meets business requirements, it is essential to get feedback and contributions from stakeholders or associates beyond the software development team, such as the marketing and sales teams. Software developers can ask for feedback from user stories and features. With Azure Test Plans, these external software development stakeholders can use the Test and Feedback extension to respond to feedback requests by collating useful diagnostic data, filing bugs, and rating requests.

➤ **Traceability:** Azure Test Plans facilitates connecting requirements and bugs to test cases and test suites. To track the quality of application requirements, tests and defects are immediately linked to the builds and requirements that are being tested.

➤ **Reporting and analysis:** Azure Test Plans includes dashboard widgets, several built-in pipeline test reports, configurable test tracking graphs, a test runs hub where you can review the results of manual and automated test executions, test data storage in the analytics service, and configurable test data reports for reporting and analysis support.

Advantages of Azure Test Plans

From the overview of how Azure Test Plans work, it is evident that this service offers lots of features to simplify testing and gathering test data on Azure DevOps. This section will further highlight some of the advantages of using Azure Test Plans.

➤ **Extensibility:** You can mix the technologies and tools you already know with the development tools that best suit your work. To give your test management life cycle the experience you require, you can utilize the Azure Test Plans feature by creating different extensions.

➤ **Platform agnostic testing:** The Azure Test Plans web portal gives you the opportunity to integrate with any modern browser. This allows all types of users to create and manage manual tests across various browsers on different devices.

➤ **Quality data collection:** During your manual tests, you can gather detailed diagnostic data using Azure Test Plans features. This consists of test impact information for your apps that are being tested, screenshots, an image action log, screen recordings, code coverage, and IntelliTrace traces. All of the bugs you create during testing automatically contain this data, making it simple for software developers to replicate the bugs and issues.

CREATING TEST PLANS AND TEST SUITES

With Azure Test Plans, you can create test suites and test plans to track manual testing for your application's requirements during a sprint. This section will cover how to manage test plans and test suites.

Test Plans

A test plan is a collection of test suites in Azure DevOps. You first create your test plan and then create multiple test suites in that plan (test suites will be covered in the next section). It is crucial for every project milestone to have its own test plan so that test teams can track requirements for each of them.

Prerequisites for creating test plans are that you have work items for your current sprint in Azure Boards (we covered Azure Boards in Chapter 3 of this book) and that you have the permissions to create test plans. Once you have successfully created the work items, you can follow the next steps to create your test plan:

1. From the Azure DevOps portal, open your project and navigate to Test Plans. Then, click New Test Plan to create a test plan for your sprint (Figure 9.1).

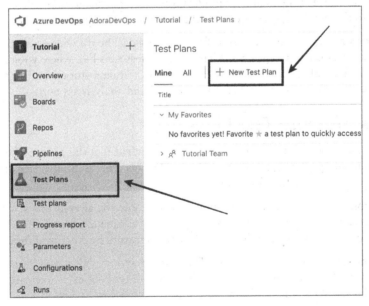

FIGURE 9.1: Navigating to Test Plans

2. In the New Test Plan window, name your test plan and verify that Area Path and Iteration are set to what you want them to be. Area Path and Iteration help you define a hierarchy of paths for your project. Area paths allow you to group work items by team, product, or feature area. Iteration paths allow you to group work into sprints, milestones, or other

event-specific or time-related periods. After filling out the fields with the right information, click Create (Figure 9.2).

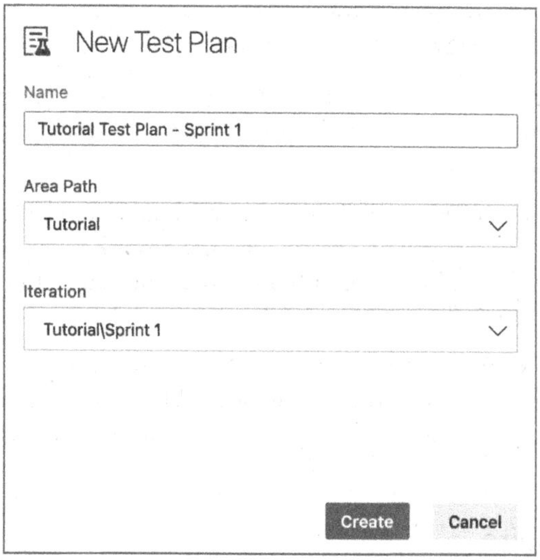

New Test Plan
Name
Tutorial Test Plan - Sprint 1
Area Path
Tutorial
Iteration
Tutorial\Sprint 1
Create
Cancel

FIGURE 9.2: Creating a new test plan

3. You have now successfully created your test plan, and you can add test suites and test cases for your project (Figure 9.3).

Tutorial Test Plan - Sprint 1
Dec 5 - Dec 12
Current
Test Suites
Tutorial Test Plan - Sprint 1
Tutorial Test Plan - Sprint 1 (ID: 15)
Define
Execute
Chart

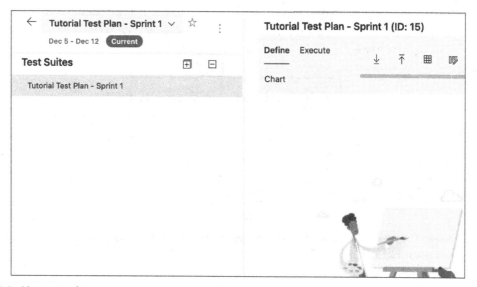

FIGURE 9.3: New test plan

Test Suites

A *test suite* is a collection of test cases in Azure DevOps. With test suites, you can group different test cases within a test plan. This grouping helps the tester to properly group all similar tests belonging to a particular scenario. There are three types of test suites:

➤ **Static suites:** A static suite is the default test suite in Azure Test Plans. With static suites, the cases have all been assigned manually. Any test case can be grouped together using these kinds of test suites.

➤ **Requirement-based suites:** A requirement-based suite is a test suite that is tethered to work items. Testers use this test suite to verify whether a work item has passed the test execution. Any test cases that have already been built and connected to that requirement get pulled in and populate your test suite.

➤ **Query-based suites:** When building a query-based test suite, you will build an ad hoc query for the types of test cases you want to include. This allows you to pull in the test cases that meet a particular criteria rather than worrying about how test cases relate to particular requirements.

Adding a Static Test Suite

This section covers the steps required to add a static test suite to your test plan.

1. In your newly created test plan, click More Options for the test suite and then select New Suite ⇨ Static Suite (Figure 9.4).

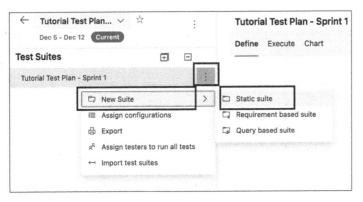

FIGURE 9.4: Selecting Static Suite

2. Name your test suite. You should now see the test suite that you created appear under the test plan (Figure 9.5).

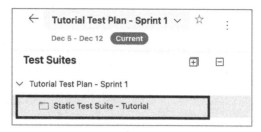

FIGURE 9.5: New static test suite

Adding a Requirement-Based Test Suite

This section covers the steps required to add a requirement-based test suite to your test plan.

1. In your newly created test plan, click More Options for the test suite and then select New Suite ⇨ Requirement Based Suite (Figure 9.6).

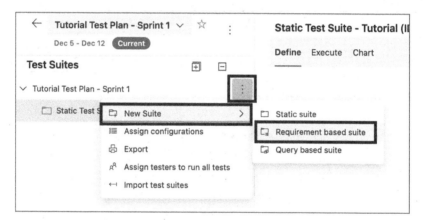

FIGURE 9.6: Selecting Requirement Based Suite

2. In the Create Requirement-Based Suites window, add one or more clauses to filter work items based on the sprint iteration path. Run the query to view the matching backlog entries (Figure 9.7).

3. Select the work items you want to test in this sprint from the list the query returned. Click Create Suite to create a requirement-based suite for each work item (Figure 9.8).

4. You should now see a test suite for each work item (Figure 9.9).

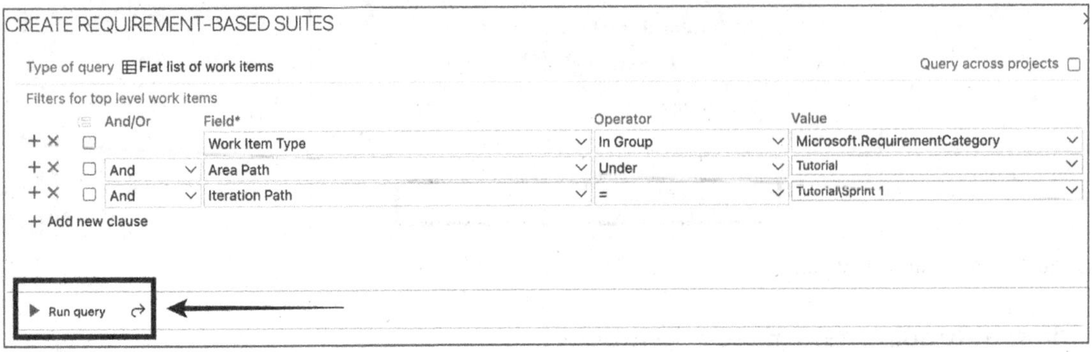

CREATE REQUIREMENT-BASED SUITES

Type of query ⊞ Flat list of work items

Query across projects ☐

Filters for top level work items

	And/Or		Field*		Operator		Value	
+× ☐			Work Item Type	∨	In Group	∨	Microsoft.RequirementCategory	∨
+× ☐	And	∨	Area Path	∨	Under	∨	Tutorial	∨
+× ☐	And	∨	Iteration Path	∨	=	∨	Tutorial\Sprint 1	∨

+ Add new clause

▶ Run query ↻ ⬅

FIGURE 9.7: Filter requirement

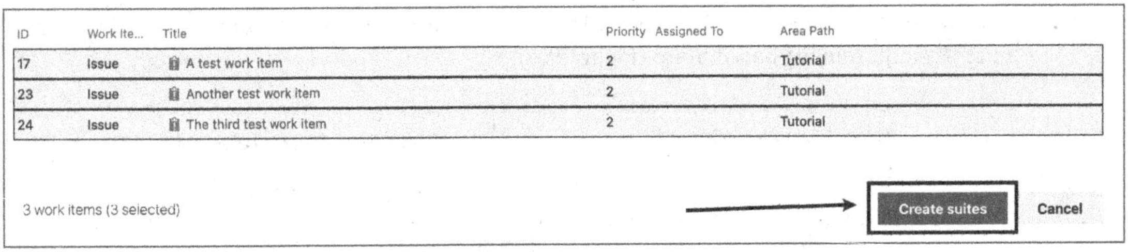

ID	Work Ite...	Title	Priority	Assigned To	Area Path
17	Issue	🗒 A test work item	2		Tutorial
23	Issue	🗒 Another test work item	2		Tutorial
24	Issue	🗒 The third test work item	2		Tutorial

3 work items (3 selected)   ➡   [Create suites]   Cancel

FIGURE 9.8: Creating the requirement-based suites

> ∨ Tutorial Test Plan - Sprint 1
>
>   🖿 24 : The third test work item
>
>   🖿 23 : Another test work item
>
>   🖿 17 : A test work item

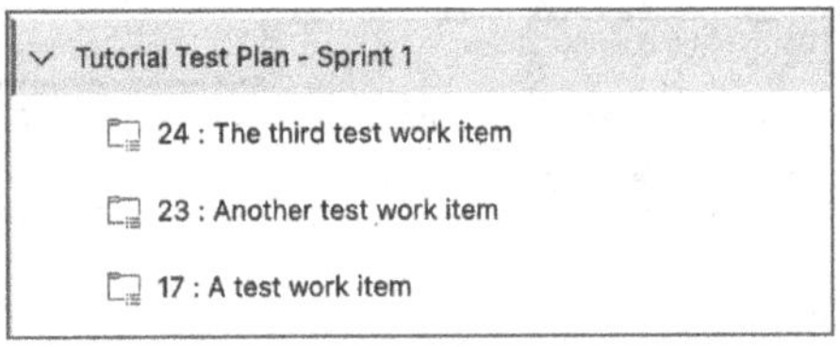

FIGURE 9.9: The requirement-based suites

Adding a Query-Based Test Suite

This section covers the steps required to add a query-based test suite to your test plan.

1. In your newly created test plan, click More Options for the test suite and then select New Suite ➪ Query Based Suite (Figure 9.10).

2. In the Create a Query-Based Suite window, add a query of your choice that you want to filter work items with (Figure 9.11).

   Unlike requirement-based suites, query-based suites are used to fetch work items based on search criteria as opposed to feature requirements.

3. Select the work items you want to test in this sprint from the list the query returned. Click Create Suite to create a query-based suite (Figure 9.12).

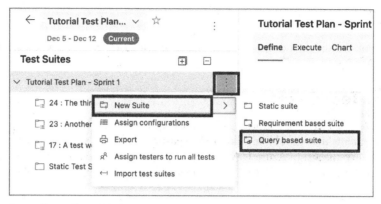

FIGURE 9.10: Selecting a Query Based Suite

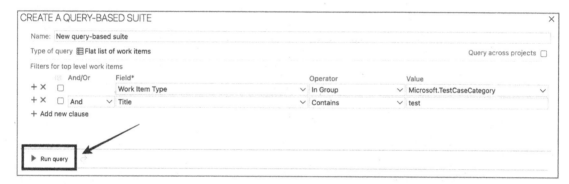

FIGURE 9.11: Query work items

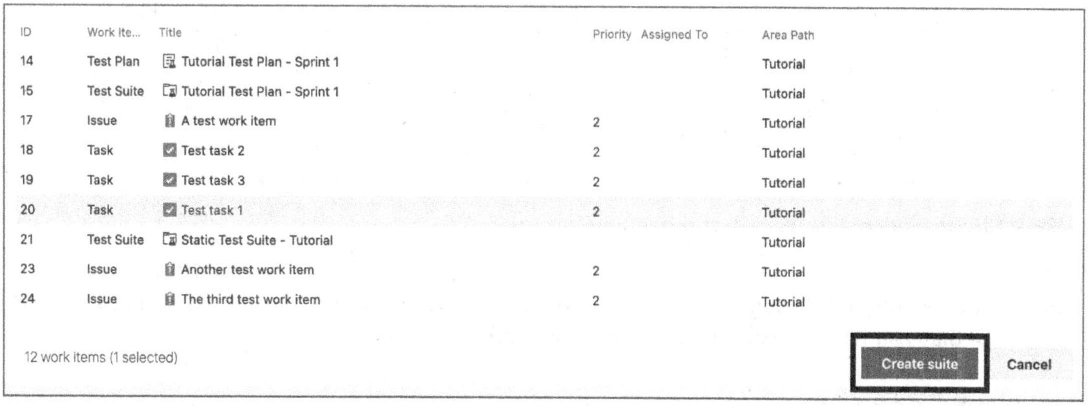

ID	Work Ite...	Title	Priority	Assigned To	Area Path
14	Test Plan	Tutorial Test Plan - Sprint 1			Tutorial
15	Test Suite	Tutorial Test Plan - Sprint 1			Tutorial
17	Issue	A test work item	2		Tutorial
18	Task	Test task 2	2		Tutorial
19	Task	Test task 3	2		Tutorial
20	Task	Test task 1	2		Tutorial
21	Test Suite	Static Test Suite - Tutorial			Tutorial
23	Issue	Another test work item	2		Tutorial
24	Issue	The third test work item	2		Tutorial

12 work items (1 selected)   Create suite   Cancel

FIGURE 9.12: Creating a query-based suite

TEST CASES

In this section, you will be introduced to the concept of test cases, and you will learn how to create them in Azure DevOps.

Overview of Test Cases

What will be tested? This is one major question a test case answers. Test cases are created to define the individual elements that should be validated to ensure that the system works accurately and passes all the quality checks. In Azure DevOps, test cases can be added to test plans or test suites. Test cases validate work items such as feature requirements or bug fixes (Figures 9.13 and 9.14).

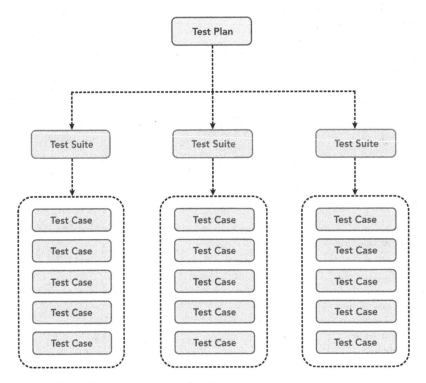

FIGURE 9.13: Structure of test plans, test suites, and test cases

This section walks you through how to create and use test cases. A prerequisite for going through this section is that you have already created a test plan and a test suite.

Creating Test Cases

You can create test cases by following the steps in this section. We will create test cases from test suites, but as mentioned earlier, you can create test cases directly from test plans if that is how you choose to structure your testing.

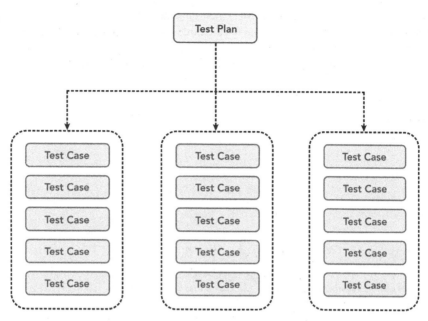

FIGURE 9.14: Structure of test plans and test cases

1. Select any of the test suites you created in the previous section and click the New Test Case button to add a test case (Figure 9.15).

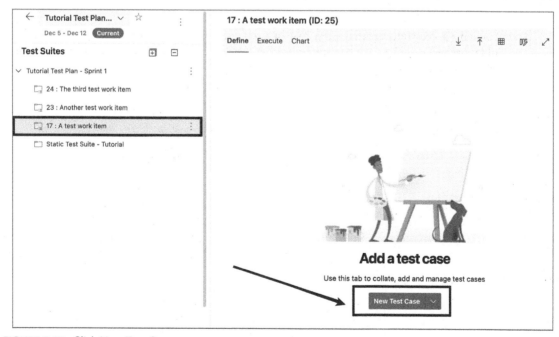

FIGURE 9.15: Click New Test Case

2.   In the Test Case window, enter a title. Click the Click Or Type Here To Add A Step option. To enable any team member to run the test, include test steps that detail the steps needed to conduct the test and the expected results. If you choose, you can include attachments in a step. Continue until you have added each of the test's steps (Figure 9.16).

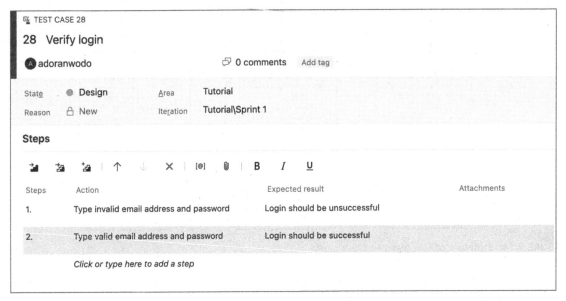

FIGURE 9.16: Test case form

3.   You have successfully created a test case in a test suite. Based on your requirements, you can add more test cases to your test suite for other elements in the feature you'd like to validate (Figure 9.17).

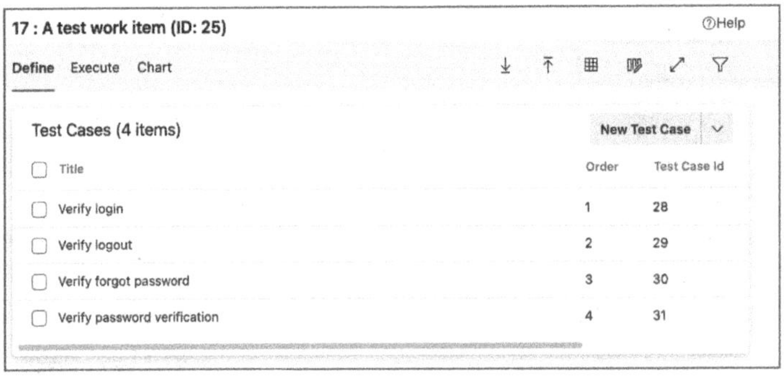

FIGURE 9.17: Test cases

CONFIGURATIONS IN TESTS

Your app will likely be installed or used by your users on a wide range of configurations, including various operating systems, web browsers, and other variations. At least a few of your tests should be run sequentially with each of those different configurations to be sure that most targeted devices for your application will run the application accurately.

Selecting which tests to run on which configurations should be based on your test plans. When running your tests, you must verify that your stages are configured for the appropriate configurations.

Combinations of configuration variable values make up a test configuration. Your configuration variables might include an operating system, browser, CPU type, and database. These are some configuration examples:

➤ Android 13

➤ Windows 10 64-bit CPU

➤ Apple iPhone 14, A15 Bionic Chipset

Creating Test Configurations

Before creating configurations, you should create the configuration variables first. Then combine multiple variable values to create a configuration. To do this for your test suites, follow these steps:

1. From the Azure DevOps web portal, select Test Plans ➪ Configurations. Click the + icon, and select New Configuration Variable (Figure 9.18).

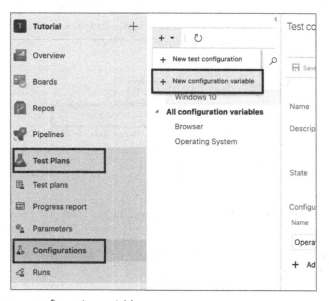

FIGURE 9.18: Creating a new configuration variable

2. Fill out all the fields in the test configuration variable window, and click Add New Value. Add as many values as you want to the configuration variable, and then save it (Figure 9.19).

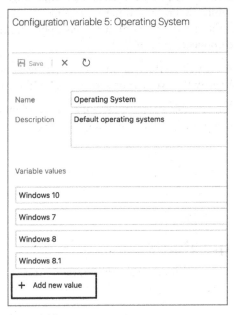

FIGURE 9.19: Adding a configuration variable

3. To create more configuration variables you might need, repeat the previous steps.

4. After creating all your configuration variables, you can now create a configuration. Click the + icon and select New Test Configuration (Figure 9.20).

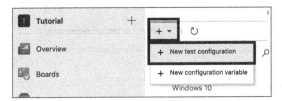

FIGURE 9.20: New configuration

5. Name the configuration and add the configuration variables you previously created. Choose a value for each variable for this configuration (Figure 9.21).

6. Once you save your new test configuration, you will have successfully created a configuration that you can assign to your test cases.

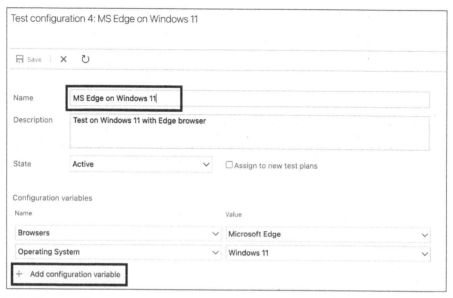

FIGURE 9.21: Adding a configuration

Assigning Test Configurations

You can assign configurations to a test suite or an individual test case. By default, test cases inherit the configurations that are assigned to its parent (test suite). Whether you assign the configurations to a test suite or test case, the steps are the same and are listed here:

1. Navigate to the test plan dashboard and find the test case (or test suite) that you want to add the configuration for. Click the menu beside it and select Assign Configurations (Figure 9.22).

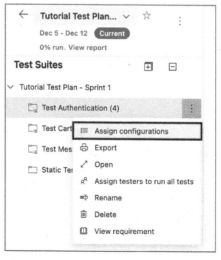

FIGURE 9.22: Assigning configurations

2. Choose the configuration you want to add and click Save (Figure 9.23).

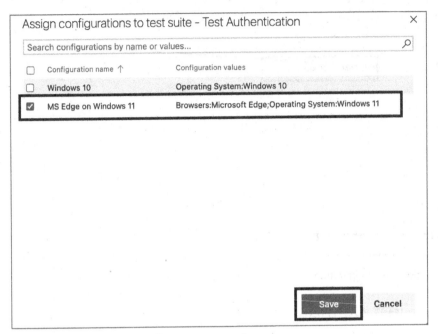

FIGURE 9.23: Selecting the previous configuration we created

3. You have now assigned a test configuration to your test suite (or test case). To validate the assignment, navigate to the Execute tab and check that the Configuration column has the right values like in Figure 9.24.

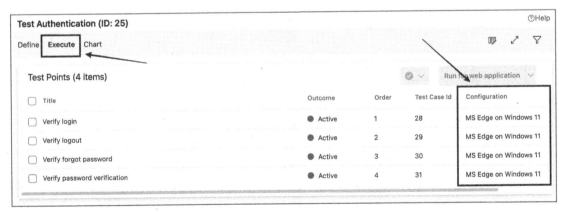

FIGURE 9.24: Verifying the assigned configurations

RUNNING MANUAL TESTS

Throughout this chapter, you have set up test plans, test suites, test cases, and configurations and assigned those configurations to test cases. These activities are building blocks for running manual tests. In this section, you will see how to run tests with this setup and track test results.

Running Tests with Configurations

Prior to this section, you created test configurations and assigned them to test cases. To run a test with your configurations, you should set up a testing platform for the configuration. For example, if you created a configuration with Windows 11 as your test operating system and Microsoft Edge as your test browser, set up a computer with these features for testing. You can use a virtual machine to do this. Once your setup is complete, follow these steps:

1. Choose a test to run that is assigned this configuration. You can run for a web application, desktop application, or other options (Figure 9.25).

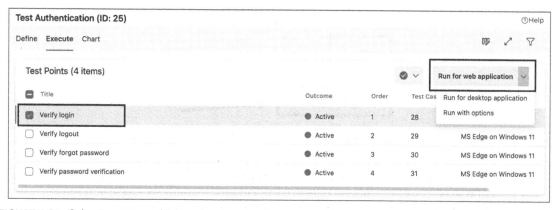

FIGURE 9.25: Selecting a manual test

2. When you click the Run button, a pop-up window appears with the list of actions to perform for that particular test. As execution goes on, you can pass or fail each test step based on whether the expected result was reached. The status bar at the bottom also has a configuration reminder; that way, you are prompted to run the right test cases in the right environment (Figure 9.26).

Viewing Manual Test Results

After executing and recording the results of your manual tests, team members who have access to the web portal can view the test results by following these steps:

1. Open the Charts page for your test suite, select New, and select New Test Result Chart (Figure 9.27).

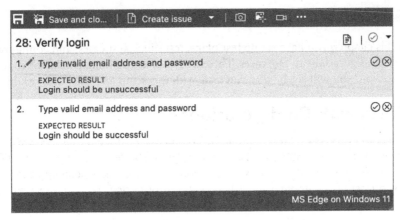

FIGURE 9.26: Test runner window

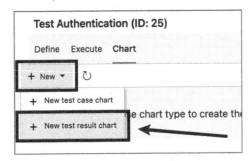

FIGURE 9.27: Selecting New Test Result Chart

2. Select the type of chart you want (e.g., a pie chart) and choose how you want to group your test results. You can group by configuration, failure type, outcome, priority, resolution, run by, run type, or suite. In Figure 9.28, results are grouped by outcome, and you can see that two tests passed, one test failed, and one test hasn't run yet. This gives internal stakeholders a graphic view of test performance, and teams can go back in future sprints to make the application better (Figure 9.28).

RUNNING AUTOMATED TESTS FROM TEST PLANS

Azure Test Plans also has the functionality to automate test cases and run them within the test plans environment. This can be useful for QA testers who are not familiar with running tests in build and release pipelines. Test Plans allows flexibility in the scheduling of automated tests, and they can be run on demand as opposed to in the build or release pipeline after certain steps and criteria have been validated. With test plans, you can also rerun a few tests that fail due to infrastructure issues without having to trigger an entire pipeline run again.

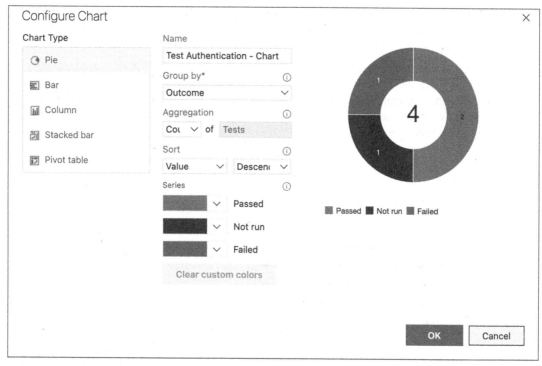

FIGURE 9.28: Test result chart

To rerun automated tests from test plans, you are required to have a test plan, an application in development (you will be testing this), and a build pipeline. A prerequisite to running these automated tests in test plans is that you set up the environment first.

Setting Up Your Environment for Automated Tests

You can set up your environment for automated tests by following these steps:

1. Select Test Plan Settings from the options on the test plan page (Figure 9.29).

FIGURE 9.29: Selecting Test Plan Settings

2. Select the build pipeline that creates builds that contain the test binaries in the Test Plan Settings dialog. The system will then use the most recent build whenever tests are run, or you can choose a specific build number to test.

    To run automated tests from test plans in Azure Test Plans, you will need a release pipeline that was built using the Test Run For Test Plans template. If you already have a release pipeline that was built using this template, select it before choosing the stage in the release pipeline where the tests will be run. If not, click the + button to build a pipeline for a release using that template (Figure 9.30).

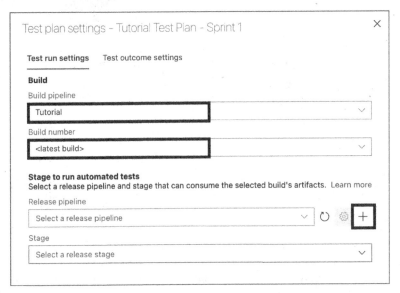

FIGURE 9.30: Test plans settings

3. Chapter 8 covered release pipelines, so we will skip many of the steps. After creating the custom release pipeline, fill out the fields and save the pipeline. Your task should look similar to Figure 9.31.

4. After successfully creating your release pipeline, add it in your test plan settings and save your settings (Figure 9.32).

Running the Tests

After successfully setting up your environment to run automated tests with Azure Test Plans, you can run the tests by following these steps:

1. Select a test suite that includes the automated tests by opening the test plan in the Test Plans web portal.

2. In the Execute tab, select the test you want to run, click the Run drop-down, and select Run With Options (Figure 9.33).

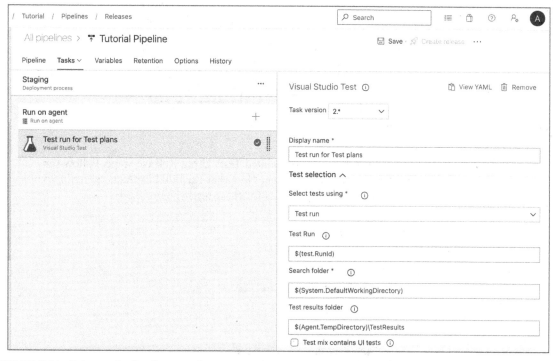

FIGURE 9.31: Release pipeline for test plans

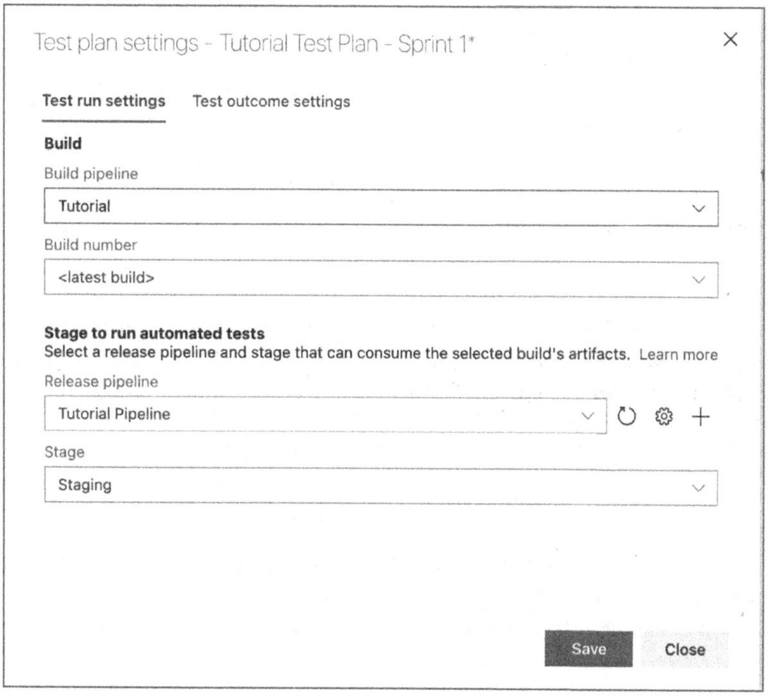

FIGURE 9.32: Test plan settings (with release pipeline details)

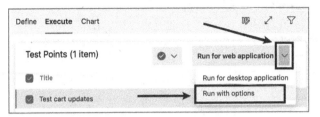

FIGURE 9.33: Selecting automated tests to run

3. In the Run With Options tab, select Automated Tests Using Release Stage. Follow the instructions, and click Run when you finish. Note that the build artifacts created by your build pipeline must include the test binaries for these tests (Figure 9.34).

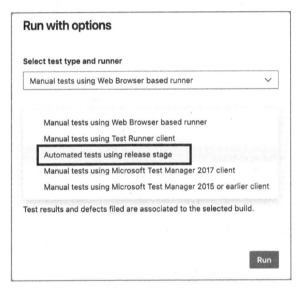

FIGURE 9.34: Running automated tests

4. During execution, the system validates the stage to guarantee that the Test Run For Test Plans task is present and has valid configurations. The system also checks the user's authorization to create a release for the specified pipeline, creates a test run, and then initiates the creation of a release to the stage.

SUMMARY

With Azure Test Plans, quality assurance teams can utilize the powerful tools provided by Azure Test Plans to promote quality and teamwork throughout the development process. Azure Test Plans is a simple-to-use test management tool that offers all the mechanisms necessary for running different application tests.

Azure Test Plans supports different types of testing goals by combining different testing tools, progress reports, and more. These goals are manual testing, exploratory testing, user acceptance testing, automated testing, stakeholder feedback, traceability, reporting, and analytics.

Some examples of Azure Test Plans include extensibility, platform agnostics testing, and quality data collection.

A test plan is a collection of test suites in Azure DevOps. You first create your test plan and then create multiple test suites in that plan (test suites will be covered in the next section). A test suite is a collection of test cases in Azure DevOps. With test suites, you can group different test cases within a test plan. This grouping helps the tester to properly group all similar tests belonging to a particular scenario. Azure Test Plans has three types of test suites: static suites, requirement-based suites, and query-based suites. Test cases are created to define the individual elements that should be validated to ensure that the system works accurately and passes all the quality checks.

Your app will likely be installed or used by your users on a wide range of configurations, including various operating systems, web browsers, and other variations. As a result, some tests should be run with each of those different configurations to validate the application's accuracy.

With Azure Test Plans, you can run and see execution data for manual and automated tests. To run automated tests, you need a release pipeline with a Test Run For Test Plans task.

Chapter 10 will cover infrastructure automation on Azure and how you can deploy your applications infrastructure using Azure Pipelines.

10

Infrastructure Automation with Azure Pipelines

This chapter covers infrastructure automation on Azure and how you can deploy your applications infrastructure using Azure Pipelines.

What You Will Learn in This Chapter

➤ Overview of Infrastructure Automation

   ➤ Types of Infrastructure as Code

   ➤ Benefits of Infrastructure as Code

➤ Infrastructure Automation Tools on Azure

   ➤ Azure Resource Manager Templates

   ➤ Azure Bicep

➤ Using Azure Bicep in Azure Pipelines

   ➤ Setting up Azure Bicep on your computer

   ➤ Azure Bicep Templates Overview

   ➤ Azure Bicep Templates in Azure Pipelines

➤ Summary

OVERVIEW OF INFRASTRUCTURE AUTOMATION

Infrastructure automation is the process of using software tools and methods to automate the provisioning and administration of your application's cloud infrastructure. Some of these tools include scripts and programming languages. This process may involve installing and configuring servers, networking hardware, and other resources. Infrastructure automation aims to increase the efficiency and repeatability of managing and maintaining application infrastructure while reducing human intervention. The goal is to lower the possibility of mistakes and errors. Organizations can save time and money by automating the provisioning and management of their infrastructure. They can also ensure that their infrastructure is consistently configured and complies with best practices and industry standards.

The infrastructure of applications was manually configured by software development teams prior to infrastructure automation. This methodology meant that to set up your infrastructure for any application, you would need to go to the cloud provider's website, choose the resources you wanted to create, follow the configuration steps, and then complete your setup. You had to go through the same steps to reprovision the infrastructure for a similar environment.

Manual infrastructure configuration has these disadvantages:

➤ **Time consuming:** Application infrastructure configuration done manually can take a long time for large and complex distributed applications. This time is because many of these systems' components, such as servers, networking hardware, and other hardware and software, require individual configuration and management. Many manual tasks, such as setting up each component, configuring its settings, and ensuring it integrates with the rest of the system, are necessary to accomplish the configuration. In addition, as the application grows, the time and effort needed to configure and maintain large and complex infrastructure resources will also increase.

➤ **Error prone:** Because of a large number of manual steps and processes prone to human error, manual configuration is more prone to errors and mistakes than automated configuration. Manually configuring application infrastructure increases the potential for mistakes, such as typing an incorrect application setting or forgetting to configure a crucial component. These errors can cause system outages, security flaws, and inconsistencies across application environments.

➤ **Inability to scale:** Because it takes a lot of time and effort to keep up with the frequent updates and changes that these systems require, manually configuring infrastructure for large, quickly expanding systems can be difficult. This difficulty makes the manual configuration approach unscalable, especially when the system has a lot of intricate components that need to be configured and maintained. An ideal situation would be managing infrastructure for a service deployed to more than 10 regions. In these circumstances, manual configuration can become overwhelming and challenging to track, resulting in errors and other issues that affect the system's dependability and performance.

Infrastructure as code (IaC) is an infrastructure automation technique that helps teams manage their application infrastructure using source code and other software development tools. For the rest of this chapter, we will discuss infrastructure as code tools on Azure and how to integrate them with Azure DevOps.

Types of Infrastructure as Code

There are two approaches for infrastructure as code: the imperative and declarative approaches. This section will cover both approaches in detail.

Imperative Infrastructure as Code

Imperative infrastructure as code refers to a particular type of infrastructure automation where the infrastructure is defined and managed with imperative programming patterns.

The imperative infrastructure as code approach answers these two questions:

➤ What actions do I want to perform?

➤ How do I want to perform those actions?

As a result, an imperative IaC infrastructure is provisioned using commands that specify what action the system should perform one after the other. When handling complicated or unique scenarios, this approach gives the administrator fine-grained control over the infrastructure.

REQUESTING BREAKFAST: AN IMPERATIVE APPROACH

Imagine you wanted to instruct a system to make you breakfast. Using the imperative approach, you would itemize all the steps needed to make the breakfast in the correct order. These steps can be as follows:

➤ Take out two slices of bread.

➤ Toast the bread.

➤ Take out two eggs.

➤ Fry the eggs.

➤ Take out one piece of bacon.

➤ Fry the bacon.

➤ Bring out a plate from the shelf.

➤ Put the toast, eggs, and bacon on the plate.

➤ Take out a tea mug.

➤ Pour hot water into the mug.

➤ Put a tea bag into the mug.

➤ Serve breakfast.

You can achieve imperative infrastructure as code on Azure with the `az cli` commands.

```
az webapp create -g testResourceGroup -p testHostingPlan -n testWebApp

az webapp update -g testResourceGroup -n testWebApp --set tags
.environment=development
```

The previous code snippet uses the imperative approach to create and update a web application on Azure. The first statement prompts Azure to create a web app called `testWebApp`. It also specifies that this web app should use the `testHostingPlan` app service plan and exist in the `testResourceGroup` resource group. After creating the web app, the next statement prompts Azure to update the web app with a tag that sets the value of `environment` to `development`.

Declarative Infrastructure as Code

Declarative infrastructure as code is based on the idea that instead of writing step-by-step scripts or manually configuring resources, you should define the desired state of your infrastructure using a declarative language.

Declarative IaC enables you to describe the final appearance of your infrastructure rather than the creation process. As a result, you can concentrate on specifying the desired outcome while the underlying infrastructure is automatically provisioned and managed to achieve it.

A declarative IaC tool, for instance, could be used to specify the desired state for a server's operating system, security configurations, and installed software. The IaC tool will automatically provision and configure the necessary resources to match that state when you apply that desired state to your infrastructure. This can help you save time and effort and make it simpler for you to manage and maintain your infrastructure over time.

Collaboration with others is more straightforward, and you can guarantee that your infrastructure is always up-to-date and consistent by using declarative IaC's versioning and change tracking capabilities. In environments where infrastructure is constantly changing, this strategy may be helpful.

REQUESTING BREAKFAST: A DECLARATIVE APPROACH

Imagine you wanted to instruct a system to make you breakfast. Using the declarative approach, you would specify the type of statement you want, and the system would sort out the rest.

The following statement is a way to declaratively specify the type of breakfast you want:

> "I want a breakfast plate with two slices of toast, two eggs, one piece of bacon, and a cup of tea."

This is very different from the imperative IaC approach that requires listing the approach in steps.

The following code snippet shows the desired state of an Azure Storage Account infrastructure using a declarative IaC tool for Azure:

```
resource storageAccount 'Microsoft.Storage/storageAccounts@2019-06-01' = {
  name: storageAccountName
  location: 'westus'
  kind: 'StorageV2'
```

```
    sku: {
      name: 'Standard_LRS'
      tier: 'Standard'
    }
  }
```

Based on the properties set in this code snippet, the automation tool will create a storage account called `storageAccountName` in `westus`. The storage account will be a `StorageV2` account using the `Standard_LRS` SKU. This is the current desired state of the storage account. However, if new requirements come along that require the software development team to update the location and add tags for the storage account, they can do so by updating the code, as illustrated here:

```
resource storageAccount 'Microsoft.Storage/storageAccounts@2019-06-01' = {
  name: storageAccountName
  location: 'westus3'
  kind: 'StorageV2'
  sku: {
    name: 'Standard_LRS'
    tier: 'Standard'
  }
  tags: {
    env: 'Development'
  }
}
```

In the previous code snippet, the storage account properties have been updated. The location is now `westus3`, and a `tag` was added. The automation tool can verify the change in the infrastructure's state and update the infrastructure to match the new state without the software developer specifying the step-by-step changes required.

Benefits of Infrastructure as Code

Adopting infrastructure as code tools come with various benefits that you will learn about in this section.

➤ **Version control:** You can store IaC code in a version control system like Git, which keeps track of file changes and enables team collaboration on the same codebase. It is possible to track changes made to the infrastructure over time, go back to earlier versions if necessary, and work together on the codebase.

➤ **Reusability:** Many organizations have different environments for testing, staging, and production. It is possible to build identical infrastructure with IaC code in all the environments. This approach guarantees consistency and lowers the chance that errors or other problems will arise because of infrastructure dissimilarities. Because the infrastructure is already set up and configured in a consistent manner, using IaC code to create identical infrastructure in various environments can also make it simpler to migrate applications and services between environments. This process saves time and can help to simplify the development and deployment methodologies.

➤ **Streamlined engineering practices:** Like application source code, software development teams can design, version, test, and roll back their IaC code. This approach makes it easy to use software architecture and programming principles in infrastructure engineering, which promotes convention and consistency across the board.

➤ **Documentation:** Software development teams can document the different components and relationships found within the infrastructure, as well as the configuration and settings for each component, by using IaC code to define and configure the infrastructure. This process can be helpful in large organizations with complicated infrastructure where it can be challenging to keep track of all the various parts and their interactions. Since everyone can refer to the IaC code to understand the infrastructure configuration and how it is supposed to operate, using IaC makes it simple to troubleshoot problems and spot potential issues in infrastructure declarations.

➤ **Idempotency:** IaC enables idempotency, which is the ability of a system or procedure to return the same output on repeated executions. To ensure that the infrastructure is dependable and stable over time and to make it simpler to troubleshoot problems and spot potential issues, promoting idempotency is a critical component of IaC. By using IaC to deploy the infrastructure consistently and predictably, errors or other problems caused by changes to the infrastructure are less likely to occur.

INFRASTRUCTURE AUTOMATION TOOLS ON AZURE

The Azure deployment and management service is called Azure Resource Manager. It offers a management layer that enables you to add, edit, and remove resources in your Azure account. Azure has two tools for declarative IaC, namely, Azure Resource Manager (ARM) templates and Azure Bicep. This section will explain these tools in detail.

Azure Resource Manager Templates

ARM templates are a way to create and manage Azure resources using a declarative approach. The resources that should be created, along with their attributes and dependencies, are specified in ARM templates, which are written in JSON.

The reusable and modular nature of ARM templates makes it simple to share and use them in various contexts. This makes it possible to develop a library of ARM templates that can be used to deploy and manage common Azure resources, including virtual machines, storage accounts, and networks. The following code snippet shows a sample ARM template for an Azure Storage Account:

```
{
  "$schema": "https://schema.management.azure.com/schemas/2019-04-01/
deploymentTemplate.json#",
  "contentVersion": "1.0.0.0",
  "parameters": {
    "storagePrefix": {
      "type": "string",
      "minLength": 3,
      "maxLength": 11
    },
```

```json
    "storageSKU": {
      "type": "string",
      "defaultValue": "Standard_LRS",
      "allowedValues": [
        "Standard_LRS",
        "Standard_GRS",
      ]
    },
    "location": {
      "type": "string",
      "defaultValue": "[resourceGroup().location]"
    }
  },
  "variables": {
    "uniqueStorageName": "[concat(parameters('storagePrefix'),
uniqueString(resourceGroup().id))]"
  },
  "resources": [
    {
      "type": "Microsoft.Storage/storageAccounts",
      "apiVersion": "2022-05-01",
      "name": "[variables('uniqueStorageName')]",
      "location": "[parameters('location')]",
      "sku": {
        "name": "[parameters('storageSKU')]"
      },
      "kind": "StorageV2",
      "properties": {
        "supportsHttpsTrafficOnly": true
      }
    }
  ],
  "outputs": {
    "storageEndpoint": {
      "type": "object",
      "value": "[reference(variables('uniqueStorageName')).primaryEndpoints]"
    }
  }
}
```

Usually, an ARM template's structure consists of the following components:

- ➤ **Schema:** This component declares that the file is a deployment template file.

- ➤ **Parameters:** Examples of these values include the name of a resource or the size of a virtual machine, which can be specified when the template is deployed. The template can be modified using parameters to fit different scenarios or environments.

- ➤ **Variables:** These are the values that can be used in the template to make complicated expressions simpler or to prevent repeating the same value repeatedly. Constants or expressions that are evaluated at runtime can both be defined as variables.

- ➤ **Resources:** These are the Azure resources that the template will create, such as web apps, storage accounts, or databases. A JSON object that includes the resource's type, name, and properties defines each resource.

➤ **Outputs:** These are values returned after the successful deployment of the template, such as the hostname of a web app. Outputs can pass information from the deployed resources to other processes.

Azure Bicep

Azure Bicep is a Resource Manager template language that declaratively deploys Azure resources. Azure Bicep is a domain-specific language that exists only for creating and managing Azure resources, so it cannot work as a standard programming language for writing applications. Regardless of your prior knowledge of other programming languages, Azure Bicep is simple to comprehend and learn. Its templates support all resource types, API iterations, and properties. The following code snippet is an Azure Bicep template that defines an Azure storage account:

```
param location string = resourceGroup().location

var storageAccountName = 'teststorage'
var storageAccountSku = 'Standard_RAGRS'

resource storageAccount 'Microsoft.Storage/storageAccounts@2022-05-01' = {
  name: storageAccountName
  location: location
  kind: 'StorageV2'
  sku: {
    name: storageAccountSku
  }
  properties: {
    accessTier: 'Hot'
    supportsHttpsTrafficOnly: true
  }
}

output storageAccountId string = storageAccount.id
```

AZURE BICEP VS. ARM TEMPLATES

Azure Bicep provides a syntax simpler than ARM templates for resource declaration. The two code snippets declared so far in this section are code snippets to create storage accounts with ARM templates and Azure Bicep. You'll notice that the Azure Bicep code is shorter in size. The syntax is more uncomplicated to read and understand, and there are no complicated expressions like the JSON ARM template.

How Azure Bicep Works

When you deploy a resource or set of resources to Azure, you send the Bicep template to the Azure Resource Manager, which still needs JSON templates. Your Bicep template is converted into a JSON template by the built-in tooling for Bicep. This process is called code *transpilation*. Once the *transpiled* code gets to the Resource Manager, operations to create, update, or delete Azure resources based on the state of the Bicep file will commence (Figure 10.1).

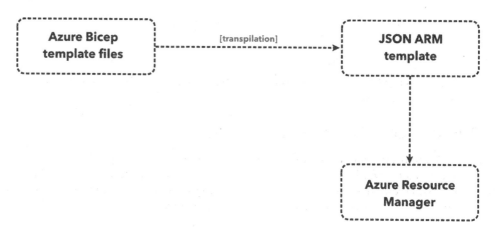

FIGURE 10.1: How Azure Bicep works

Benefits of Azure Bicep

Using Azure Bicep comes with various benefits that you will learn about in this section.

➤ **Integration with Azure services:** Azure Bicep deployments integrate seamlessly with different Azure services including Azure Pipelines, a tool you can customize for your infrastructure deployments.

➤ **Simpler syntax:** Bicep files are shorter and simpler to read when compared to ARM templates. No prior programming experience is necessary for Bicep.

➤ **Code reuse:** Complex template deployments can be broken down into smaller module files and referenced in the primary template. These modules offer simpler management and better reusability, and you can share them across different teams.

USING AZURE BICEP IN AZURE PIPELINES

This section will cover how to set up Azure Bicep and use Azure Bicep with Azure Pipelines for infrastructure deployments.

Setting Up Azure Bicep on Your Computer

Before doing infrastructure automation in the Azure Pipelines, you will need to set up Azure Bicep on your local computer. This involves installing the Azure CLI and the Azure Bicep extension.

1. Visit the Azure CLI installation website (`learn.microsoft.com/en-us/cli/azure/install-azure-cli?view=azure-cli-latest`) to learn how to install the Azure CLI for your specific machine. If you install version 2.20.0 (or later) of the Azure CLI, you also get the Bicep CLI as part of the installation.

2. After installing the Azure CLI, you can verify your Azure Bicep version by running the following command:

```
az bicep version
```

You now successfully have the Azure and Bicep CLI installed. In the next section, you will learn the basic concept of Azure Bicep templates.

Azure Bicep Templates Overview

An Azure Bicep template is a file that allows you to define and deploy Azure resources using a clear and straightforward syntax. You use the Azure Bicep language to create Azure Bicep templates that specify the resources you want to create or modify in your Azure environment. The following code snippet shows an Azure Bicep template for creating a web app:

```
resource appServicePlan 'Microsoft.Web/serverFarms@2022-03-01' = {
  name: 'test-plan'
  location: 'westus3'
  sku: {
    name: 'F1'
  }
}

resource appServiceApp 'Microsoft.Web/sites@2022-03-01' = {
  name: 'test-web-app'
  location: 'westus3'
  properties: {
    serverFarmId: appServicePlan.id
    httpsOnly: true
  }
}
```

In an Azure Bicep template, you can specify resource declarations for one or more Azure resources. Each resource declaration defines a particular Azure resource you want to create or change.

Each resource declaration is made up of the following elements:

➤ A resource type, which defines the kind of Azure resource you want to create (e.g., `Microsoft.Web/sites@2022-03-01`)

➤ A resource name, which identifies the resource within the Azure Bicep template (e.g., `appServiceApp`)

➤ A set of properties that defines the specific attributes of the Azure resource you want to manage (e.g., the server farm ID, the app settings, etc.)

Once you have written your Azure Bicep template, you can use it to deploy your Azure resources using Azure Pipelines, and you can also automate the deployment process.

Azure Bicep Templates in Azure Pipelines

Beyond source code deployments and running tests, you can also set up your release pipeline to do infrastructure deployments. This section will cover the steps required for automating infrastructure deployments using Azure Pipelines.

Pipeline Authentication

The Azure Resource Manager determines whether the resources exist before deploying the template. If not, the Resource Manager creates them. If any are present already, the Azure Resource Manager guarantees they have the same configuration as specified in the template.

Because they access and alter your Azure resources, each of these operations needs permission. You must have permission to create deployments to deploy Azure Bicep templates. Deployments are resources with the Microsoft.Resources/deployments type.

When doing infrastructure deployments from your local computer, you typically use your user account and browser-based authentication. When you submit a deployment, Azure checks to verify that your identity has the permissions required to carry out the tasks your Azure Bicep template specifies. When you switch to a pipeline, you have to use a different type of authentication method because the release pipeline handles deployments without your identity. You can give your pipeline permissions for creating resources through a service connection.

To create a service connection, follow these steps:

1. In your Azure DevOps project dashboard, click Project Settings and click the Service Connections tab. A window will appear to create a service connection (Figure 10.2).

FIGURE 10.2: Navigating to new service connection

2.   In the New Service Connection pop-up, select Azure Resource Manager and click Next (Figure 10.3).

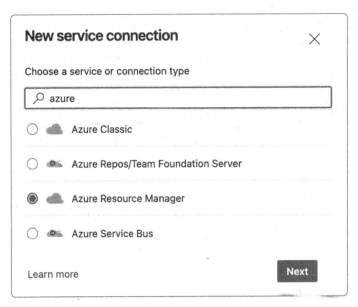

FIGURE 10.3: New Service Connection pop-up

3. Next, select Service Principal (Automatic) as the authentication method (Figure 10.4).

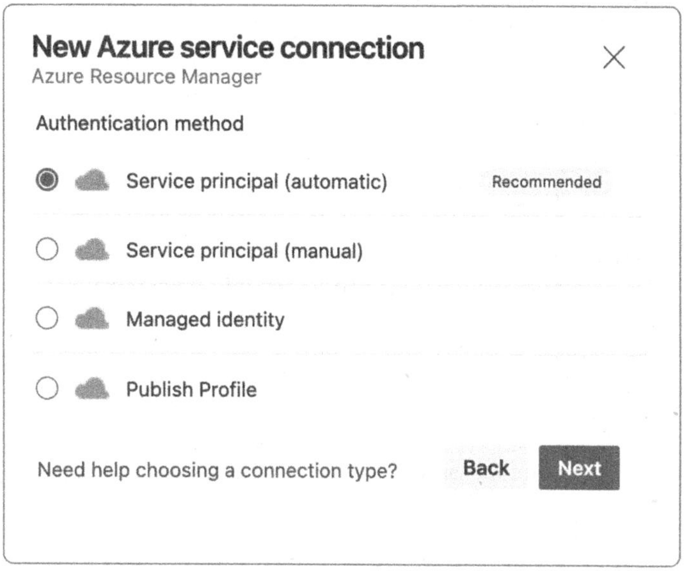

New Azure service connection
Azure Resource Manager

Authentication method

◉ 🌩 Service principal (automatic)   Recommended

○ 🌩 Service principal (manual)

○ 🌩 Managed identity

○ 🌩 Publish Profile

Need help choosing a connection type?   **Back**   **Next**

FIGURE 10.4: Choosing an authentication method

4. Next, choose the subscription scope level and select the Azure subscription and resource group that you want this service connection to be valid for. Name your service connection, add an optional description, and remember to grant access permissions to all pipelines. After filling out this information, save your settings (Figure 10.5).

Once you have successfully created the service connection, it will show up in your list of service connections, and you will be able to use it for your pipeline deployments.

Deploying Azure Bicep Templates Using the Pipeline

This section covers the steps required to deploy Azure Bicep templates using Azure Pipelines. To do this, you must have a repository that contains a Bicep template. Follow these steps to automate the deployment of your Azure Bicep scripts:

1. Navigate to the Azure Pipelines dashboard and connect to Azure Repos Git (Figure 10.6).

2. Next, choose your repository and configure your pipeline. Choose the Starter pipeline (Figure 10.7). You will update it with YAML scripts later.

3. At this stage, Azure Pipelines will create a placeholder pipeline YAML file for you. Replace the pipeline steps with the following script:

```
- task: AzureResourceManagerTemplateDeployment@3
  inputs:
    connectedServiceName: 'DeploymentConnection'
    location: 'westus3'
    resourceGroupName: test-rg
    deploymentName: 'TestDeployment'
```

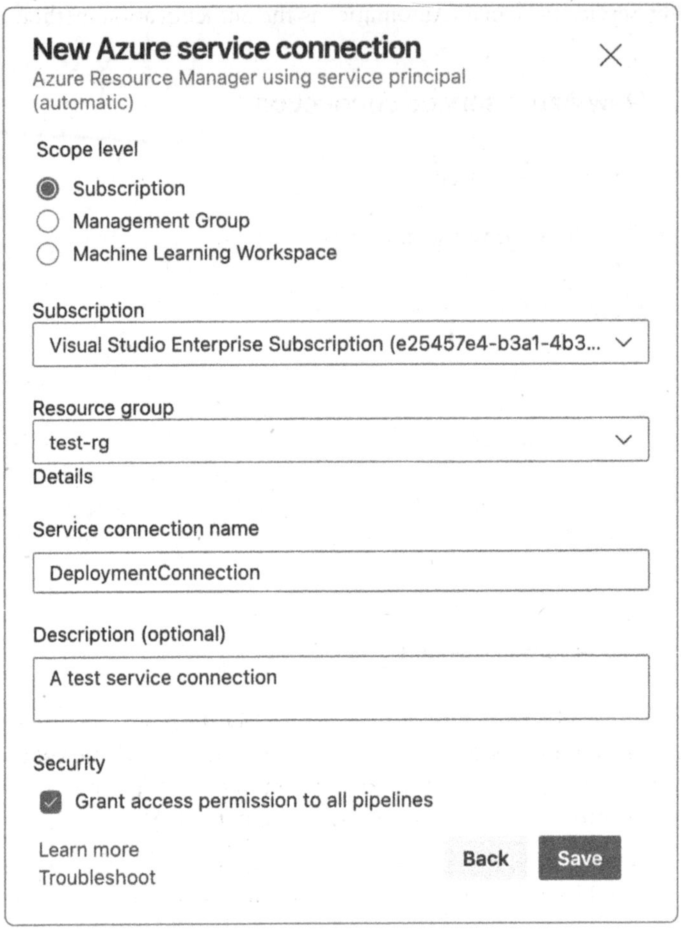

FIGURE 10.5: Service connection details

In the previous snippet, `AzureResourceManagerTemplateDeployment@3` is specified in the first line. It instructs Azure Pipelines to use version 3 of the task with the name `AzureResourceManagerTemplateDeployment` for this step. When using the `AzureResourceManagerTemplateDeployment` task, you must specify inputs to instruct the task on what to do. Some of the inputs are listed here:

➤ **connectedServiceName** is the name of the service connection to use. Here, you can put the name of the service connection you created in the previous section. The task logs into Azure using the service connection when it first launches. This means that `az login` is not required.

➤ **location** defines the location of your resource group.

➤ **resourceGroupName** defines the name of the resource group that the Azure Bicep template will be deployed to.

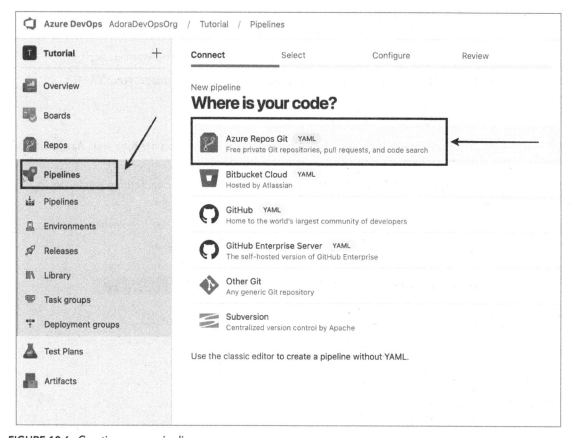

FIGURE 10.6: Creating a new pipeline

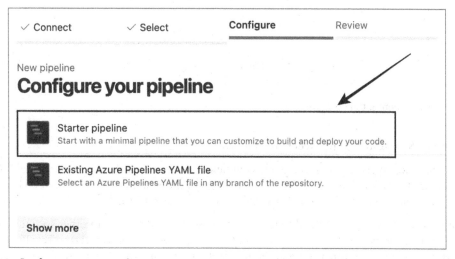

FIGURE 10.7: Configuring your pipeline

➤ **deploymentName** defines the identifier of the Azure Bicep deployment on the Azure Portal. This can be a unique string like the build number.

➤ **csmFile** defines the path to the Azure Bicep template that you want to deploy.

If your Azure Bicep template also has parameters, you can add this to your YAML:

```
overrideParameters: >
  -parameterName parameterValue
```

`overrideParameters` includes a list of parameters you want to pass into your Azure Bicep template at deployment time.

After adding the YAML script to your pipeline, you should have something similar to Figure 10.8.

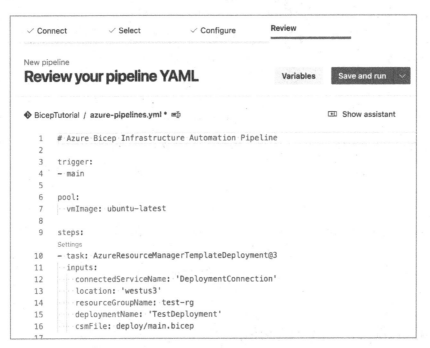

FIGURE 10.8: Deployment pipeline YAML file

4. Click Save And Run to execute the pipeline.

5. Once your pipeline has successfully completed, you can visit the Deployments tab in the Azure Portal to verify your deployment. To go to the Azure Portal, visit (portal.azure .com) and sign in with your Microsoft account (Figure 10.9).

You have successfully explored the different ways to use Azure Pipelines. In other sections, you created build and release pipelines, and you used your Azure Pipelines with Azure Test Plans. Now, you've also seen how to automate infrastructure deployments in Azure Pipelines. To take this a step further, you can deploy more complex infrastructure to multiple environments and see what the results will be.

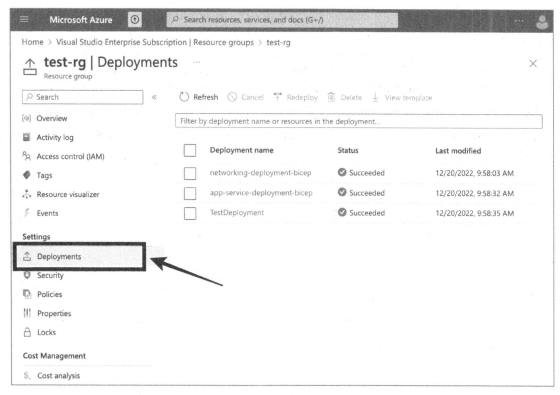

FIGURE 10.9: Verifying your deployment

SUMMARY

Infrastructure automation is the process of using software tools and methods to automate the provisioning and administration of your application's cloud infrastructure.

The infrastructure of applications was manually configured by software development teams prior to infrastructure automation. This methodology meant that to set up your infrastructure for any application, you would need to go to the cloud provider's website, choose the resources you wanted to create, follow the configuration steps, and then complete your setup. Some disadvantages of manual infrastructure configuration were that it was error prone, time consuming, and did not scale.

There are two approaches for infrastructure as code: imperative and declarative. Imperative IaC infrastructure is provisioned using commands that specify what action the system should perform one after the other. Declarative IaC infrastructure is based on the idea that instead of writing step-by-step scripts or manually configuring resources, you should define the desired state of your infrastructure using a declarative language.

Azure has two tools for declarative IaC, namely, Azure Resource Manager (ARM) templates and Azure Bicep. ARM templates are a way to create and manage Azure resources using a declarative approach. The resources that should be created, along with their attributes and dependencies, are specified in ARM templates, which are written in JSON.

Azure Bicep is a domain-specific language that exists for creating and managing Azure resources.

When doing infrastructure deployments from your local computer, you typically use your user account and browser-based authentication. When you switch to a pipeline, you have to use a different type of authentication method because the release pipeline handles deployments without your identity. You can give your pipeline permissions for creating resources through a service connection.

You can automate your applications Azure Bicep infrastructure deployment with Azure Pipelines.

Chapter 11 will introduce a sample project with different exercises that will enable you to practice the various Azure DevOps tools and services you have learned so far.

11

Exercise—Practice Using Azure DevOps Tools

This chapter introduces a sample project with different exercises that will enable you to practice the various Azure DevOps tools and services you have learned so far.

Chapter Exercises

➤ Introducing the Sample Application

    ➤ Create a Fork of the Project

    ➤ Clone Your Fork Locally

➤ Importing the Repository from GitHub to Azure Repos

➤ Using Azure Boards to Manage Work Items

➤ Committing Code That Adds New Features

➤ Building the Code in Azure Pipelines

➤ Deploying the Code

➤ Summary

INTRODUCING THE SAMPLE APPLICATION

This section will introduce the sample application for the practice Azure DevOps exercises. First, you'll set up any text editor or integrated development environment (IDE) so that you can build the project on your computer and work with the source files.

The application is a sample library application with two variations. One is written in .NET, and the other is in Node.js. So, you can choose to work on whichever version is more comfortable for you.

Create a Fork of the Project

Making a fork allows you to work with and edit the source files, which is the first step of using a project in Git. A *fork* is a copy of a GitHub repository. You can modify the fork as much as you'd like without impacting the original project because the fork exists in your account.

Let's fork the SampleLibraryApp web project into your GitHub account.

1. In your web browser, navigate to GitHub (github.com) and sign in.

2. Navigate to the SampleLibraryApp project (github.com/AdoraNwodo/ SampleLibraryApp).

3. Select Fork (Figure 11.1).

FIGURE 11.1: Forking the project

4. You will see a form similar to the one in Figure 11.2. Fill in the form and create a fork of the project.

> ### Create a new fork
>
> A *fork* is a copy of a repository. Forking a repository allows you to freely experiment with changes without affecting the original project.
>
> ⓘ Single sign-on to see more options for organizations within the **Microsoft Open Source** enterprise.
>
> **Owner ***   **Repository name ***
>
> [_____] **/** [SampleLibraryApp   ✓]
>
> By default, forks are named the same as their upstream repository. You can customize the name to distinguish it further.
>
> **Description** (optional)
>
> [_____]
>
> ☑ **Copy the** main **branch only**
>   Contribute back to AdoraNwodo/SampleLibraryApp by adding your own branch. Learn more.
>
> ⓘ You are creating a fork in the adorahack organization.
>
> [Create fork]

FIGURE 11.2: Create fork form

Clone Your Fork Locally

You can download or clone a copy of the SampleLibraryApp project to your local computer so that you can work with it now that you have successfully forked the project to your GitHub account. Clones are copies of repositories, much like forks are. A repository can be cloned so that you can make changes, check that they work as expected, and then upload the updated version to GitHub. To copy the project to your computer, follow these steps:

1. Navigate to your fork of the SampleLibraryApp project on GitHub.

2. Select Code from the command bar. A pane with tabs for the various types of cloning appears, showing the Clone option. The URL can be copied to your clipboard by clicking the Copy icon next to it on the HTTPS tab (Figure 11.3).

FIGURE 11.3: Cloning a project

3. Open your terminal window, enter `git clone`, and then paste the URL from your clipboard. It should look similar to this:

```
git clone https://github.com/<username>/SampleLibraryApp.git
```

4. After completing the cloning process, you can navigate to the project directory and on your local computer, start contributing to the project.

IMPORTING THE REPOSITORY FROM GitHub TO AZURE REPOS

In the previous section, you got introduced to the project, and you forked and cloned the GitHub Repository. The next step is to import the repository from GitHub to Azure Repos since we are working with Azure DevOps tools.

To do this, navigate to the Repos dashboard in Azure DevOps project and select Import Repository (Figure 11.4).

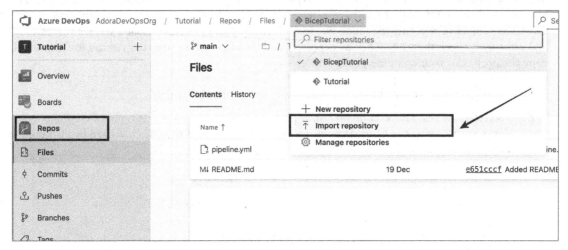

FIGURE 11.4: Importing a repository

In the Clone URL field, paste the link of the GitHub project you forked in the previous section. You should see something similar to Figure 11.5.

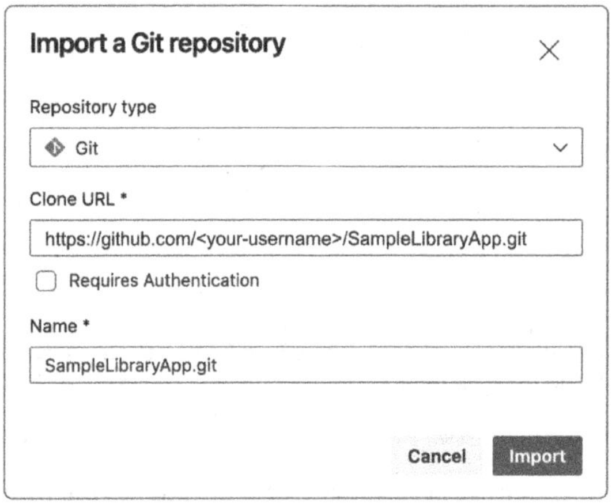

FIGURE 11.5: Import repository wizard

After successfully importing the project to Azure Repos, you should see something similar to Figure 11.6. At this point, you now have the code files in Azure and can start planning, building, testing, and releasing your project updates.

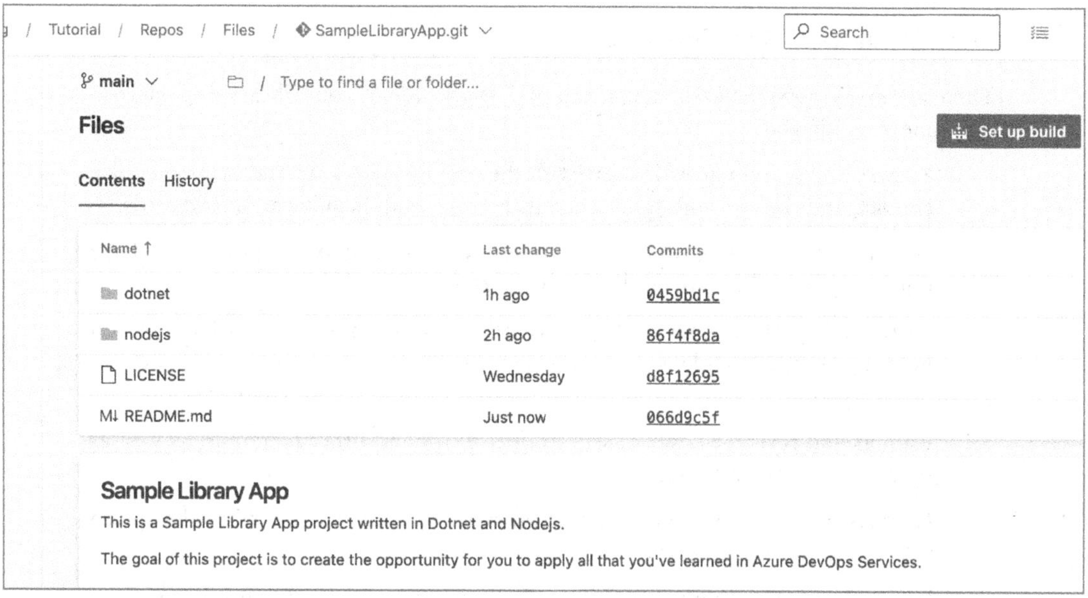

FIGURE 11.6: Azure Repos project

USING AZURE BOARDS TO MANAGE WORK ITEMS

You now have some parts of a sample library application, and you can build out features to make a complete application however you want it to be. But before building, it's important to plan the features you'd like to add to the application.

Planning software feature development requires careful consideration of a number of factors to ensure that the feature meets specific needs, is feasible to develop, and aligns with the overall goals and vision for your software. These are some of the things required in planning software feature development:

➤ Defining the issue or need the feature seeks to address. You can create your own set of features because this is a personal project. In practice, though, this might entail talking to stakeholders, such as clients or users, and doing market research to figure out what the target audience wants.

➤ Defining the feature's objectives and range of use. The feature's specific functionalities as well as any nonfunctional requirements, such as performance or usability objectives, may need to be decided upon at this point.

➤ Establishing a development schedule.

SAMPLE LIBRARY APP FEATURES

There are many possible features you can plan to include in your library app. Here are some to guide you:

➤ **Browse and search:** Provide users with the option to look up and browse books, ebooks, audiobooks, and other content by title, author, subject, or keywords.

➤ **History:** Provide users with the ability to view a history of the books they have borrowed as well as any books they have returned.

➤ **Alerts and notifications:** Send users notifications when items they have put on hold become available or when items they have checked out are due to be returned.

➤ **Ratings and reviews:** Enable users to rate books and other materials, as well as read other users' ratings and reviews.

➤ **Helpdesk:** Allow users to chat with library staff or other users inside the app to ask questions or get assistance.

➤ **Social sharing:** Enable users to post their recommended reading lists to social media sites for friends and family to see.

➤ **Personalized suggestions:** Make suggestions for books and other materials based on a user's reading preferences and history.

➤ **Account management:** Enable users to view and change their account status, update their personal information, and manage their preferences inside the app.

For this exercise, do the following tasks:

➤ Practice adding work items to your Azure Boards project. These work items can include user stories, bugs, and tasks. Each work item should be tagged, have an appropriate description, and be linked to a parent (or child). Work items should also be assigned to you. Creating and populating these fields appropriately makes it easier to organize and track these work items.

➤ Practice adding some low-priority work items to the backlog so that you can plan for them later.

➤ Practice using queries to filter and group work items based on various criteria (e.g., assigned to a particular person, belonging to a particular iteration, etc.).

➤ Practice creating iterations (i.e., sprints) in Azure Boards and organizing them by assigning work items, specifying start and end dates, and monitoring progress.

When you create different work items, Azure Boards should look similar to Figure 11.7.

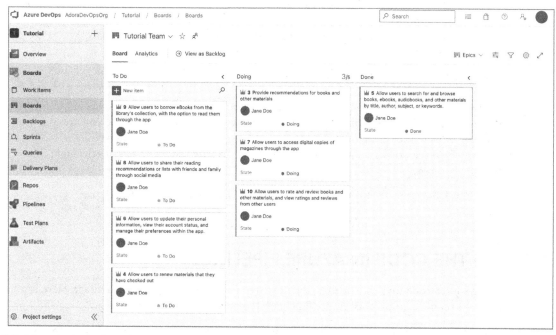

FIGURE 11.7: Azure Boards

EXERCISE SUCCESS METRICS

To measure success, you should have a backlog of work items that contain different features that you have planned for your application. You should also set up sprints and individual tasks within those sprints. These sprints will guide you in planning for specific tasks within a time frame, and each work item will help you know what task you are working on at any given time.

Check out Chapter 3 for an Azure Boards refresher. You might need it for this exercise.

COMMITTING CODE THAT ADDS NEW FEATURES

After planning the different software features, the next step will be to add those features to the application source code. Here is a list of tasks that you can use to practice Azure Repos and add code for new features:

➤ Add code changes to the repository and commit them using Git commands.

➤ Use branches in Azure Repos to isolate code changes and manage development workflows. This could include tasks such as creating and merging branches and resolving merge conflicts.

➤ Use pull requests in Azure Repos to review code changes. This could include creating and reviewing pull requests and using the built-in code review tools.

➤ Set up and integrate Azure Repos with Azure Boards to improve traceability and collaboration. This helps track work items, pull requests, and code changes in a single place. With this, you can link pull requests and commits to different Azure Boards work items.

EXERCISE SUCCESS METRICS

To measure success, you should have created a feature branch, committed code to Azure Repos, and created a pull request that is linked to a work item. Since you are probably working on this alone, there is no need to review and merge your pull request. However, you can also decide to do that to be sure you're able to go through the entire process.

Check out Chapter 4 for an Azure Repos refresher. You might need it for this exercise.

BUILDING THE CODE IN AZURE PIPELINES

After writing source code for new features, the next step is to build the software artifact. Here is a list of tasks that you can use to practice Azure Pipelines and add code for new features:

➤ Create a new pipeline in Azure Pipelines and learn how to set up the basic pipeline settings, such as the source control repository and the build trigger. You can also explore using the classic editor to create a pipeline without YAML.

➤ Add tasks to the pipeline and configure them to perform various actions, such as building code, running tests, or deploying to a staging environment.

➤ Integrate Azure Pipelines with Azure Artifacts.

If you are using YAML for your pipeline, you can use the following code snippet to build your .NET project:

```
steps:
- task: DotNetCoreCLI@2
  displayName: Build
  inputs:
    command: build
    projects: '**/*.csproj'
    arguments: '--configuration $(buildConfiguration)' # Update this to
match your need
```

If you are using the Node.js project, you can use the following code snippet:

```
trigger:
- main

pool:
  vmImage: 'ubuntu-latest'
```

```
steps:
- task: NodeTool@0
  inputs:
    versionSpec: '16.x'
  displayName: 'Install Node.js'

- script: |
    npm install
  displayName: 'npm install'

- script: |
    npm run build
  displayName: 'npm build'
```

If you'd like to try more things, you can also add other pipeline tasks for testing, linting, and code coverage.

EXERCISE SUCCESS METRICS

To measure success, you should have created a pipeline using either YAML or the classic editor. This pipeline should be triggered when a pull request merges to the main branch. This pipeline should be able to build your source code and publish the artifacts.

Check out Chapter 5 for an Azure Pipelines refresher. You might need it for this exercise.

DEPLOYING THE CODE

The final step in this exercise is to set up automated deployments for your application. Here is a list of tasks that you can use to further practice Azure Pipelines and automate your source code deployments:

➤ Add tasks to the pipeline and configure them to deploy applications to different environments, such as staging, production, or testing environments. This helps you to learn how to configure the pipeline settings to suit the needs of the different environments.

➤ Use Azure Pipelines to deploy infrastructure as code: Azure Pipelines can be used to deploy infrastructure as code, using tools such as Azure Bicep or Azure Resource Manager (ARM) templates.

EXERCISE SUCCESS METRICS

To measure success, you should have created a release pipeline using either YAML or the classic editor. This pipeline should be triggered when a pull request merges to the main branch. This pipeline should also be able to download your source code artifacts and deploy them to different environments (e.g., staging and production).

As an extra step, you can also set up automated infrastructure as code deployments that run in the release pipeline.

Check out Chapter 8 and Chapter 10 for an Azure Pipelines refresher (code and infrastructure deployments). You might need it for this exercise.

SUMMARY

In this chapter, you were introduced to a sample library web application written in .NET and Node.js. The goal was to try to get you to use the different Azure DevOps services in a project. You were also given some sample requirements for features to plan your application. Beyond this, there were sample exercises for building, testing, and deploying your application using Azure.

Chapter 12 will highlight tips for starting a career using tools from the entire Azure DevOps ecosystem.

12

Starting a Career in Azure DevOps

This chapter will highlight tips for starting a career using tools from the entire Azure DevOps ecosystem.

What You Will Learn In This Chapter

➤ Starting an Azure DevOps Career

➤ Getting Your First Job As An Azure DevOps Engineer

➤ Finding an Azure DevOps Community Near You

➤ Summary

STARTING AN AZURE DevOps CAREER

Building a career in DevOps and getting your first job can be a rewarding and challenging journey. One reward is that it allows you to work on a broad spectrum of thrilling and impactful tech projects where you can play a crucial role in enabling organizations to deliver high-quality applications more quickly and efficiently. However, it can be challenging because it requires knowledge of different tools and technologies, and the field is also constantly evolving.

This section highlights some practical steps that can help in your journey as you try to start a career in this field.

➤ **Learn the fundamentals:** Having a solid foundation in the underlying technologies and principles of DevOps is crucial because it's such a broad field. It is essential to comprehend how computers operate to work with them. Many of these foundational concepts have been covered in this book and can help you build the required knowledge.

➤ **Build projects:** Being hands-on with the tools and services is the best way to learn Azure DevOps. Here are some ways that you can build projects that use Azure DevOps:

➤ **Create a personal project:** Consider creating a personal project, such as creating an application with your friends and utilizing Azure DevOps to manage and track your progress. This project will enable you to practice using the various Azure DevOps tools and services and see how they function in real-life situations.

➤ **Contribute to open-source projects:** Contributing to open-source projects is a great way to get hands-on experience with the tools and services since many open-source projects use Azure DevOps. You can look for open-source projects utilizing Azure DevOps and see if there are any opportunities to contribute. A good place to start is GitHub, as there are a lot of open-source projects there. You can also explore some open-source projects at `opensource.microsoft.com/projects`. This way, you get to make an impact in a real-world project and work with a diverse set of people.

➤ **Participate in a hackathon:** Participating in hackathons can be a great way to learn from and collaborate with other software developers, DevOps engineers, and other professionals who contribute to the success of a software product. It also helps you gain practical experience with Azure DevOps. See if there are any opportunities to participate by looking into hackathons in your neighborhood or virtually.

➤ **Network:** Networking with other industry professionals can be a helpful way to find out about job openings and get guidance on your career path. To meet other industry experts, contribute to online communities or go to conferences and meetups.

➤ **Get a certification:** Getting certified is not required, but it can be a good way to show prospective employers your knowledge and abilities. There are many Azure DevOps–related certifications available online, but because Microsoft developed it, I suggest the DevOps Engineer Expert certification (`learn.microsoft.com/en-us/certifications/ devops-engineer`). The combination of theoretical knowledge and real-world experience required for certifications can help you differentiate yourself from the competition.

HOW TO FIND OPEN-SOURCE AZURE DevOps PROJECTS

➤ **Search the Internet:** Open-source projects using Azure DevOps are listed in numerous online resources. You can try searching for these resources using queries like "open source projects for Azure DevOps."

➤ **Reach out to open-source organizations:** Many organizations use Azure DevOps for their open-source projects and might be interested in onboarding new contributors. You can get in touch with them directly to find out if they have any open-source projects using Azure DevOps and whether they are looking for contributors.

➤ **Reach out to open-source communities:** Developers can discuss open-source projects and share resources in different online communities. You can become part of these communities and inquire whether other participants know of any open-source projects utilizing Azure DevOps. The Azure DevOps Community on the Microsoft Community Hub (`techcommunity.microsoft.com`) is one community you can join.

➤ **Search GitHub:** Open-source projects frequently use Azure DevOps for continuous integration and delivery (CI/CD), and GitHub is a popular platform for hosting them. To locate repositories that utilize Azure Pipelines, for instance, use the search term "topic:azure-pipelines" (Figure 12.1).

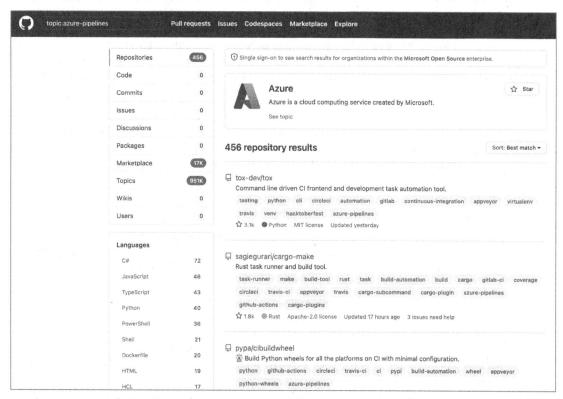

FIGURE 12.1: Sample GitHub search results for Azure Pipelines topics

GETTING YOUR FIRST JOB AS AN AZURE DevOps ENGINEER

Once you've done all the things highlighted in the previous section, you will be ready to start looking for your first opportunity. There are three things you can do to find your next opportunity as an Azure DevOps engineer.

➤ **Leverage your network:** The network you've built is important for key reasons. Building relationships, finding job opportunities, and keeping current in your industry require networking. It can help you develop relationships with experts in your field, learn about industry trends and developments, and showcase your skills and experience. Networking can also help you learn about job openings that might not be publicly advertised. Since employers frequently prefer to hire applicants who have been recommended by their employees or colleagues, networking is a common way to fill job openings. You might be able to learn about unlisted job openings and gain access to them before they are formally posted by networking with other professionals in your field.

➤ **Use job search websites:** Job search websites can be a valuable resource in your job search because they can help you find positions that fit your qualifications and experience, keep you informed of any new positions that become available, connect you with more employers, and give you access to tools that aid in your job search. In addition to letting you search for jobs based on keywords, location, and other factors, many job search websites regularly update their listings to keep you informed of any new positions that become available. You can reach more employers by using the large audience of job seekers and employers found on many job search websites. Additionally, a lot of job search websites offer tools and resources like résumé builders, job search advice, and career resources to assist you in your job search.

LinkedIn, Glassdoor, Indeed, `DevOps.com`, `DevOpsJobBoard.com`, and Arc.dev are just a few of the job search engines you can use to find Azure DevOps positions. `DevOps.com` and `DevOpsJobBoard.com` are specialized job search websites that concentrate on DevOps roles, while LinkedIn, Glassdoor, Indeed and Arc.dev are well-known job search websites that cover a wide range of industries and roles. Using keywords like "Azure DevOps," "DevOps engineer," or "Azure DevOps engineer," you can use these websites to look for Azure DevOps roles.

➤ **Attract recruiters:** Your ability to access job openings that may not be publicly advertised through recruiters can be a significant advantage in the job search process. To assist businesses in filling job openings with qualified applicants, many recruiters collaborate with them. They frequently have access to positions that are not publicly advertised. This can apply to positions that are currently being filled through personal connections, employment agencies, or positions that are not yet prepared for public posting. These kinds of job openings might not be reachable through conventional job search channels, but if a recruiter is interested in your skills and experience, they might be able to help you get to the interview stage. Additionally, a lot of great résumés can get ignored in job application portals due to the huge number of people applying. Direct involvement with a recruiter can help you skip that step and grant you the interview.

You can take multiple actions to attract recruiters to you. Being active on LinkedIn, networking, and building your professional network can all help you stand out to recruiters. You can showcase your abilities and experience on LinkedIn, making it easier for recruiters to find you and learn more about your work. Networking can also be a valuable way to attract recruiters. You can meet them online, at networking events, or through professionals in your field already in your network.

The next step after getting the interview is preparing for and ideally passing all the interview stages. You can prepare for DevOps interviews by reviewing typical Azure DevOps interview questions, reviewing your qualifications and experience, practicing with a friend or mentor, looking over the business's website and social media profiles, and being punctual on the interview day. You can feel more prepared and confident during your interview by reviewing frequently asked DevOps interview questions and practicing your responses. You can also practice answering interview questions with a friend or mentor to become more comfortable and to get feedback on your responses. Being on time can help you make a good first impression, and doing your research on the company you are interviewing with can help you tailor your responses to align with their goals and expectations.

AZURE DevOps INTERVIEW SAMPLE AREAS

Here are some areas that interview questions can come from. You should do some preparation around the following:

➤ Azure DevOps overview

➤ Continuous integration, continuous delivery, and continuous deployment

➤ Managing breaking changes

➤ Troubleshooting production issues

➤ Dependency management

➤ Security compliance

➤ Agile methodologies

➤ Handling project scope changes and requirements changes

➤ Handling project risks and issues

➤ Testing and test automation

➤ Monitoring and optimizing application performance

➤ Containerization and container orchestration tools, such as Docker and Kubernetes

➤ Infrastructure as code (IaC) tools

➤ Version control and branching strategies

➤ Build and release pipelines

➤ Deployment strategies (such as blue/green deployments or rolling deployments)

➤ Disaster recovery and business continuity planning

FINDING AN AZURE DevOps COMMUNITY NEAR YOU

Tech professionals gather in tech communities for education, networking, community building, and support. Workshops and training sessions may be available in these communities for opportunities for professional development. They can be useful for establishing valuable networking connections and for learning about new job opportunities. Tech communities can offer assistance, opportunities for collaboration, and are great places to turn to for advice on difficulties you are having at work.

Additionally, tech communities can give a sense of community and belonging and can be a great way to meet other like-minded professionals and forge connections. Joining an Azure DevOps community can be very useful in your tech career. The following tips highlight how you can find an Azure DevOps community near you:

➤ **Search the Internet:** You can find Azure DevOps communities in your area by searching online or using social media platforms. To find regional communities or meetups, for instance, type "Azure DevOps community [city name]" or "Azure DevOps meetup [city name]" into your search engine. Additionally, you might try searching for particular associations or groups, like the Azure User Group or the Azure DevOps User Group.

➤ **Connect with local tech companies:** Connecting with local tech firms can be a great way to discover local opportunities and make connections with people who are enthusiastic about Azure DevOps. Many tech firms in your area might already be utilizing Azure DevOps or other related technologies. You can meet local tech companies and find out how they use Azure DevOps by using online directories or networking events.

➤ **Use LinkedIn connections:** Connecting with other professionals who have an interest in Azure DevOps can be facilitated by using LinkedIn. To find professionals in your area who are interested in Azure DevOps, use LinkedIn's search function. You can also join LinkedIn groups or follow organizations that are specializing in Azure DevOps to stay up-to-date on industry advancements.

SUMMARY

A career in DevOps involves working on exciting tech projects and enabling organizations to deliver high-quality applications efficiently. However, it requires knowledge of various tools and technologies and is constantly evolving, making it both rewarding and challenging.

To start your career in Azure DevOps, you can learn the fundamentals of DevOps and underlying technologies, build projects using Azure DevOps (personal project, open-source, hackathons), network with other industry professionals, and contribute to online communities and attend conferences and meetups.

Obtaining an Azure DevOps certification, such as the DevOps Engineer Expert, can demonstrate your knowledge and abilities to prospective employers and help you stand out from the competition. However, certifications are not necessary.

To find your next opportunity as an Azure DevOps engineer, you can leverage your network, use job search websites, and work on attracting recruiters to you.

Tech communities can offer assistance, opportunities for collaboration, and are great places to turn to for advice on difficulties you are having at work.

To find an Azure DevOps community near you, you can search the Internet, connect with local tech companies, and make LinkedIn connections.

Chapter 13 is a summary of everything you have learned in this book.

13

Conclusion

"It is not the strongest of species that survives, nor the most intelligent that survives. It is the one that is the most adaptable to change."

—Charles Darwin

Learning a new software engineering tool or concept can be difficult because it often requires a significant investment of time and effort to acquire new knowledge and skills. But by reading *Beginning Azure DevOps,* you've shown that you're willing to put in the work and push through the hard parts. You may have encountered unfamiliar terms and concepts, struggled to understand how to use new tools, and encountered obstacles and frustrations. However, you may have overcome these obstacles and gained a better understanding of Azure DevOps tools and services. The ability to learn and adapt to new technologies is an essential skill for any technology professional, and by doing so, you have demonstrated that you have what it takes to continue to grow and develop in the field.

This book provides a comprehensive introduction to the concept of DevOps, including its history and evolution over time. You have learned about the origins of DevOps, how it emerged as a response to the challenges faced by software development teams, and how it has grown to become a widely adopted practice in the industry. You have also learned about the DevOps life cycle and the various stages involved. This includes the planning, development, CI/CD, monitoring, and feedback stages and how they are integrated and automated to improve the overall software delivery process. You also learned about the various benefits of DevOps, as well as the current state of DevOps in the industry and how it has grown to become a widely adopted practice among organizations.

You were also introduced to Azure DevOps and the different services it offers. You learned about Azure DevOps as a cloud-based platform that enables organizations to implement DevOps practices and improve the software development process. You also learned about the different Azure DevOps services such as Azure Boards, Azure Repos, Azure Pipelines, Azure Artifacts, and Azure Test Plans. These services are designed to support the different stages of the

DevOps life cycle, such as planning, development, testing, and deployment. Azure Boards, for example, enables teams to plan, track, and manage work items, while Azure Repos provides Git and Team Foundation Version Control (TFVC) for source control management. Azure Pipelines allows you to automate builds, releases, and deployments. Azure Artifacts allows you to create, host, and share packages, and Azure Test Plans provides a comprehensive testing solution. You also learned about the Azure DevOps Server, the on-premise version of Azure DevOps, which enables organizations to implement DevOps practices on their infrastructure.

This book also introduced a section of practice exercises designed to help you apply the concepts you learned about Azure DevOps. These exercises were intended to provide hands-on experience with the different services and features of Azure DevOps and to help you gain a deeper understanding of how to use the platform effectively before applying for your next role. The book not only provided technical content on Azure DevOps but also offered valuable tips and advice for those looking to start a career in this field. This includes information on how to get your first job, such as networking, building a strong portfolio, and learning the fundamentals. The goal was to provide a comprehensive learning experience for you. This included not only the technical concepts and information needed to understand and work with Azure DevOps but also the guidance and advice necessary to start building a career in this field.

I hope that this book has been a valuable resource for learning about the various Azure DevOps services and how to effectively use them in both personal and professional projects to improve your productivity and streamline your workflows. Remember, the learning journey does not end with just reading this book. It is only the beginning of your Azure DevOps journey. To fully understand and master Azure DevOps, it is important to continue to practice and work on more projects using these services. This will help you to gain hands-on experience, build your skills and knowledge, and become more proficient in using the platform. It is also important to stay up-to-date with the latest developments in Azure DevOps, and to connect with other professionals in the field to learn from their experiences and share your own. By continuing to learn and practice, you will be able to grow your knowledge and skills in Azure DevOps and increase your chances of success. I wish you all the best in your learning journey, and I hope you have a great career.

APPENDIX

REVIEW QUESTIONS

This Review Questions section provides a set of questions to reflect on the material covered in each chapter, helping you evaluate your comprehension of the concepts discussed. These questions aim to stimulate critical thinking and encourage you to analyze the information presented in the chapter. Their main objective is to assist you in identifying areas where you may require additional review or study. This section can be utilized as a self-evaluation tool and as a study aid for exams.

CHAPTER 1

1. What is DevOps?
2. Describe what existed before DevOps.
3. What is the Agile methodology?
4. List and explain the different stages in the DevOps life cycle.
5. List and explain benefits of DevOps.
6. What is the cloud?
7. What is cloud computing?
8. What is cloud engineering?
9. What is DevOps engineering?
10. What is DevSecOps?
11. What is site reliability engineering?
12. What is software as a service (SaaS)?

CHAPTER 2

1. What is Azure DevOps?
2. Describe the difference between Azure DevOps Services and Azure DevOps Server.

3. Describe the similarities between Azure DevOps Services and Azure DevOps Server.

4. What are the added benefits with using Azure DevOps Services over Azure DevOps Server?

5. What is Azure Boards?

6. What is Azure Repos?

7. What is Azure Pipelines?

8. What is Azure Test Plans?

9. What is Azure Artifacts?

10. What are the benefits of using Azure DevOps?

CHAPTER 3

1. What is an Azure DevOps organization?

2. List the different tasks you can perform in an Azure DevOps organization.

3. What is an Azure DevOps project?

4. What are the types of Azure DevOps projects?

5. What approach can be used to create more streamlined security between Azure DevOps projects?

6. What benefits does a single project provide across an organization?

7. How can teams share resources in a single project?

8. Can a single project be used for large products or services managed by multiple teams?

9. Are there any drawbacks to having a single project?

10. Can the drawbacks of a single project affect other areas such as releases, builds, and repositories?

11. What are the benefits of having multiple projects in an organization?

12. What are some reasons an organization may choose to use multiple projects?

13. List and explain the different processes supported by Azure Boards.

14. What is a work item?

15. How do backlogs help in project planning?

16. What is the product backlog?

17. What are some features of backlogs that make project planning hassle-free?

18. What is an Azure DevOps project board?

19. What is a sprint?

20. How can you use queries in Azure Boards?

21. What is a delivery plan?

22. What are the benefits of using delivery plans?

23. How can delivery plans help product teams plan specific milestones?

CHAPTER 4

1. What is version control, and how does it relate to software development?

2. What is a version control system, and how does it work?

3. How do version control systems help software teams manage changes to source code over time?

4. What is the purpose of code reviews in the context of version control?

5. What is a distributed version control system?

6. What is a centralized version control system?

7. What is a lock-based version control system?

8. What is an optimistic version control system?

9. Describe the history of version control.

10. What are the benefits of version control?

11. What is Git?

12. What is a branch?

13. What is a snapshot?

14. What is a Git repository?

15. What is a commit?

16. What does it mean to clone a repository?

17. What does it mean to pull from a repository?

18. What does it mean to push to a repository?

19. What are Git tags?

20. Describe an annotated Git tag.

21. Describe a lightweight Git tag.

CHAPTER 5

1. What is continuous integration?

2. What are the advantages of continuous integration?

3. What is continuous deployment?

4. What are the advantages of continuous deployment?

5. What is continuous delivery?

6. What is the difference between continuous delivery and continuous deployment?

7. What are Azure Pipelines?

8. List and explain some Azure Pipeline features.

9. What is a target environment?

10. What is a staging environment?

11. What is a canary environment?

12. What is a production environment?

13. List and explain the two ways to define an Azure pipeline.

14. What is a pipeline stage?

15. What is a pipeline job?

16. What is a pipeline task?

17. How are a stage, a job, and a task related in the pipeline?

18. What is a pipeline agent?

19. Describe the two types of agents you can define in Azure Pipelines.

20. What is an agent pool?

21. Describe the two types of agent pools you can define in Azure Pipelines.

22. List six images supported by Microsoft-hosted agents.

23. What is a personal access token?

24. Describe YAML and what it is used for in the pipeline.

CHAPTER 6

1. What is software testing?

2. What is quality assurance?

3. How did software testing come to be?

4. What is continuous testing?

5. List and explain the importance of software testing.

6. What are unit tests?

7.   What are the advantages of writing good unit tests?

8.   What are integration tests?

9.   What are the advantages of writing good integration tests?

10.   What are smoke tests?

11.   What are the advantages of writing good smoke tests?

12.   What are regression tests?

13.   What are the advantages of writing good regression tests?

14.   What are end-to-end tests?

15.   What are the advantages of writing good end-to-end tests?

16.   List and explain other types of software tests.

17.   Highlight and explain the steps for running software tests.

CHAPTER 7

1.   Why is it important to store shared source code?

2.   What is an artifact repository?

3.   What is the primary purpose of an artifact repository?

4.   What are build artifacts?

5.   What are deployment artifacts?

6.   What are Azure Artifacts?

7.   What are the different types of packages supported by Azure Artifacts?

8.   What are symbols?

9.   Explain what Azure Artifacts feeds are.

10.   What is a project-scoped feed?

11.   What are the features of a project-scoped feed?

12.   What is an organization-scoped feed?

13.   What are the features of an organization-scoped feed?

14.   What are public feeds?

15.   Describe the Azure Artifact feed views.

16.   What are upstream sources?

17.   What are the advantages of upstream sources?

CHAPTER 8

1. What is the continuous deployment methodology, and how does it relate to code updates?
2. How are code updates automatically released into production environments in the continuous deployment methodology?
3. How does automation help with releasing updates to production environments?
4. What are the advantages of continuous deployment?
5. What are the potential drawbacks of continuous deployment?
6. Describe the importance of automation.
7. List and describe some of the important tools that should exist in the continuous deployment workflow.
8. How does continuous delivery work?
9. What are the advantages of continuous delivery?
10. What are blue-green deployments?
11. What are the advantages of release pipelines?
12. As part of every software release, what are the steps that Azure Pipelines must run?
13. What is a release?
14. What is a multistage release pipeline?

CHAPTER 9

1. Describe Azure Test Plans.
2. List and describe some testing goals supported by Azure Test Plans.
3. What is exploratory testing?
4. When is exploratory testing ideal?
5. What are the advantages of using Azure Test Plans?
6. What is a test plan?
7. What is the prerequisite for creating a test plan in Azure Test Plans?
8. What is a test suite?
9. What is a static test suite?
10. What is a requirement-based suite?
11. What is a query-based suite?

12.   What is a test case?

13.   Highlight the importance of test configurations.

14.   How can you run automated tests using Azure Test Plans?

CHAPTER 10

1.   What is infrastructure automation, and how does it relate to the provisioning and administration of cloud infrastructure?

2.   What tasks does infrastructure automation involve?

3.   What are the benefits of automating infrastructure provisioning and management?

4.   How was the infrastructure of applications configured prior to infrastructure automation?

5.   What are some disadvantages of manual configuration for infrastructure?

6.   Describe imperative infrastructure as code.

7.   Describe declarative infrastructure as code.

8.   Explain Azure Resource Manager (ARM) Templates and how they can be used to define infrastructure.

9.   Explain Azure Bicep and how it can be used to define infrastructure.

10.   What are the benefits of Azure Bicep?

11.   What is a service connection?

12.   Describe how to set up and automate infrastructure deployments in Azure Pipelines.

CHAPTER 12

1.   What are some of the rewards of building a career in DevOps?

2.   How does a career in DevOps enable you to play a crucial role in organizations?

3.   What are some of the challenges of building a career in DevOps?

4.   What type of knowledge is required for a career in DevOps?

5.   How is the field of DevOps constantly evolving?

6.   What are some practical steps that can help in your journey as you try to start a career in DevOps?

7.   What are the three things you can do to find your next opportunity as an Azure DevOps engineer?

8.   What are the tips you can use to find an Azure DevOps community near you?

REFERENCES

There are a vast number of resources available for Azure DevOps, and it would be impractical to list every single one in this appendix. Instead, the resources included here are carefully selected to provide additional depth and various perspectives on the information presented throughout this book. These resources can be used to supplement your understanding and aid in your learning journey with Azure DevOps. They offer different ways of approaching the material, which will enhance your overall understanding and help you to apply the concepts to real-world scenarios.

A Word About the Internet   The Internet is a valuable resource for obtaining current and easily accessible information. It offers a wide range of knowledge that can be utilized to learn new skills, solve problems, and stay up-to-date with the latest advancements in specific fields. The most efficient way to access this information is through popular search engines such as Google or Bing. Searching on these platforms is straightforward, and even if you are new to using search engines, you can find instructions on how to search by clicking the Help button on each search page. Once you enter the keywords or phrases you want to research, you will be presented with a list of websites that are relevant to your search query.

Information About Azure DevOps Services Updates   There are several sources that you can use to stay informed about updates and new features for Azure DevOps Services. The Azure DevOps Services documentation (`docs.microsoft.com/en-us/azure/devops/index`) is a great resource for learning about new updates and features. The Azure DevOps Services forum (`developercommunity.visualstudio.com`) is a community-driven platform where users can ask questions and share information about updates and new features. The Azure DevOps Services Twitter account (`twitter.com/AzureDevOps`) is also a great way to stay updated on the latest features and updates on the platform. Lastly, Azure DevOps Services road map (`docs.microsoft.com/en-us/azure/devops/index`) provides a high-level overview of upcoming features and updates to the platform. By keeping an eye on these sources, you can stay up-to-date on the latest updates and features for Azure DevOps Services.

Community Forums   Community forums are a valuable resource for obtaining information about current trends and best practices in the DevOps field. These forums provide a platform for individuals to share their experiences, ask questions, and learn from others who are working in the same field. They can be a great source of information, particularly when it comes to troubleshooting and identifying new trends in DevOps. Some community forums are member-only sites, which means that you need to register and be approved to access the content. However, even these member-only forums often have useful information available to nonmembers. Community forums are also a good way to network with others in the same field, which can lead to potential job opportunities or collaborations. Additionally, many of these forums are moderated by experts in the field, which ensures that the information shared is accurate and up-to-date.

As previously noted, other sources of information for DevOps and Azure DevOps Services are publicly available. Also, keep in mind that the presence of these resources on the list does not serve as validation of the information they provide. They are simply offered as options for further study if you want more detailed information on a particular subject. The list has been organized and grouped according to their specific function to make it easier to find what you're looking for.

> **NOTE** At the time of writing this book, the URLs listed in this appendix were active and can be accessed. However, because of the constant changes that happen on the Internet, it's possible that some of these links may have been modified or no longer exist. The URLs are included as a reference point, but it's recommended to verify for updates or changes before attempting to use them. It's also possible that some of these URLs might not be accessible in certain regions or require a subscription to access the content. It's important to keep in mind that these URLs are offered as suggestions for further reading, but they cannot be guaranteed to be accurate or up-to-date.

DevOps, SITE RELIABILITY ENGINEERING, AND PLATFORM ENGINEERING

DevOps, site reliability engineering (SRE), and platform engineering all deal with the management and creation of technology systems. The resources in these fields generally include information on automation, continuous integration and delivery, infrastructure as code, and monitoring and logging. These resources are intended for both individual contributors, such as developers and system administrators, as well as managers who oversee the implementation of these practices in an organization. They offer advice on the best methods, tools, and techniques to enhance the efficiency, dependability, and scalability of technology systems. Furthermore, these resources can assist professionals in staying current with the latest industry trends and advancements.

BOOKS

Nichole Forsgren, PhD, Jez Humble, and Gene Kim. *Accelerate: Building and Scaling High Performing Technology Organizations*. Portland, OR: IT Revolution, 2018.

Gene Kim, Jez Humble, Patrick Debois, and John Willis. *The DevOps Handbook: How to Create World-Class Agility, Reliability, and Security in Technology Organizations*. Portland, OR: IT Revolution, 2016.

Nenne Adaora Nwodo. *Cloud Engineering for Beginners*. Lagos, NG: Etchwise Consulting Limited, 2021.

Sanjeev Sharma. *The DevOps Adoption Playbook: A Guide to Adopting DevOps in a Multi-Speed IT Enterprise*. Hoboken, NJ: John Wiley & Sons, Inc., 2017.

Gene Kim, Kevin Behr, and George Spafford. *The Phoenix Project: A Novel about IT, DevOps, and Helping Your Business Win*. Portland, OR: IT Revolution, 2018.

Jennifer Davis, and Ryn Daniels. *Effective DevOps: Building a Culture of Collaboration, Affinity, and Tooling at Scale.* Sebastopol, CA: O'Reilly Media, 2016.

Emily Freeman. *DevOps for Dummies.* Hoboken, NJ: John Wiley & Sons, Inc., 2019.

Betsy Beyer, Niall Richard Murphy, David K. Rensin, Kent Kawahara, and Stephen Thorne. *The Site Reliability Workbook: Practical Ways to Implement SRE.* Sebastopol, CA: O'Reilly Media, 2018.

Joakim Verona. *Practical DevOps.* Birmingham, UK: Packt Publishing Ltd, 2016.

Julien Vehent. *Securing DevOps: Security in the Cloud.* Shelter Island, NY: Manning, 2018.

Martyn Coupland. *DevOps Adoption Strategies: Embracing DevOps Through Effective Culture, People, and Processes.* Birmingham, UK: Packt Publishing Ltd, 2021.

Mirco Hering. *DevOps for the Modern Enterprise: Winning Practices to Transform Legacy IT Organizations.* Portland, OR: IT Revolution, 2018.

David Gonzalez. *Implementing Modern DevOps: Enabling IT organizations to deliver faster and smarter.* Birmingham, UK: Packt Publishing Ltd, 2017.

Ethan Thorpe. *DevOps: A Comprehensive Beginners Guide to Learn DevOps Step by Step.* 2019.

Cindy Sridharan. *Scaling Microservices: Platform Engineering for Distributed Systems.* Sebastopol, CA: O'Reilly Media, 2018.

Len Bass, Ingo Weber, and Liming Zhu. *DevOps: A Software Architect's Perspective.* Boston, MA: Addison-Wesley Professional, 2015.

ARTICLES

SRE vs. DevOps vs. Platform Engineering, www.thenewstack.io/sre-vs-devops-vs-platform-engineering

The Basics of DevSecOps Adoption, www.devops.com/the-basics-devsecops-adoption

How DevOps is evolving into Platform Engineering, www.redhat.com/architect/devops-enterprise-architect-2022

Building a Business Case for SAP DevOps Automation, www.basistechnologies.com/blog/building-a-business-case-for-sap-devops-automation

How to be the right person for DevOps, www.opensource.com/article/20/3/devops-relationships

What is DevOps Culture?, www.atlassian.com/devops/what-is-devops/devops-culture

Microsoft Learn: DevOps, learn.microsoft.com/en-us/devops/what-is-devops

IBM: DevOps Fundamentals,

www.ibm.com/topics/devops

GitLab: DevOps Fundamentals, about.gitlab.com/topics/devops

AZURE DevOps SERVICES

These resources are some of the many related to the advanced concepts of Azure DevOps including documentation, tutorials, and sample code to help users learn how to apply the various tools and services.

BOOKS

Sjoukje Zaal, Stefano Demiliani, and Amit Malik. *Azure DevOps Explained: Get Started with Azure DevOps and Develop Your DevOps Practices*. Birmingham, UK: Packt Publishing Ltd, 2020.

Ashish Raj. *Demystifying Azure DevOps Services: A Guide to Architect, Deploy, and Administer DevOps Using Microsoft Azure DevOps Services (English Edition)*. Uttar Pradesh, India: BPB Publications, 2021.

Chaminda Chandrasekara, and Pushpa Herath. *Hands-on Azure Repos: Understanding Centralized and Distributed Version Control in Azure DevOps Services*. New York City, USA: Apress, 2019.

Jeffrey Palermo. *.NET DevOps for Azure: A Developer's Guide to DevOps Architecture the Right Way*. New York City, USA: Apress, 2019.

Soni Mitesh. *Hands-on Azure DevOps*. Uttar Pradesh, India: BPB Publications, 2020.

Soni Mitesh. *Implementing DevOps with Microsoft Azure*. Birmingham, UK: Packt Publishing Ltd, 2017.

Ambily K K. *Azure DevOps for Web Developers: Streamlined Application Development Using Azure DevOps Features*. New York City, USA: Apress, 2020.

Scott Guthrie, Mark Simms, Tom Dykstra, Rick Anderson, and Mike Wasson. *Building Cloud Apps with Microsoft Azure: Best Practices for DevOps, Data Storage, High Availability, and More*. Redmond, WA: Microsoft Press, 2014.

Mikael Krief. *Learning DevOps: A Comprehensive Guide to Accelerating DevOps Culture Adoption with Terraform, Azure DevOps, Kubernetes, and Jenkins*. Birmingham, UK: Packt Publishing Ltd, 2022.

ARTICLES

Getting started with Azure DevOps, learn.microsoft.com/en-us/azure/devops/get-started

Working with Azure DevOps, www.simplilearn.com/what-is-azure-devops-article

Azure DevOps on Perficient, blogs.perficient.com/tag/azure-devops

What Is Azure DevOps? Services, Examples, and Best Practices, www.codefresh.io/learn/azure-devops

Azure DevOps: The Next Big Thing in Application Lifecycle Management, www.simplilearn.com/azure-devops-article

Azure DevOps: A Beginner's Guide, www.bmc.com/blogs/azure-devops

Azure DevOps Services, azure.microsoft.com/en-us/products/devops

Azure Artifacts documentation, `learn.microsoft.com/en-us/azure/devops/artifacts`

Azure Boards documentation, `learn.microsoft.com/en-us/azure/devops/boards`

Azure Pipelines documentation, `learn.microsoft.com/en-us/azure/devops/pipelines`

Azure Repos documentation, `learn.microsoft.com/en-us/azure/devops/repos`

Azure Test Plans documentation, `learn.microsoft.com/en-us/azure/devops/test`

Analytics and Reporting in Azure DevOps, `learn.microsoft.com/en-us/azure/devops/report`

Azure DevOps Settings and Usage documentation, `learn.microsoft.com/en-us/azure/devops/organizations`

Cross-service, Azure, and GitHub integration documentation, `learn.microsoft.com/en-us/azure/devops/cross-service`

Azure Boards Configuration & Customization documentation, `learn.microsoft.com/en-us/azure/devops/reference`

Azure DevOps Wikis, search, & navigation documentation, `learn.microsoft.com/en-us/azure/devops/project`

Marketplace & Extensibility documentation, `learn.microsoft.com/en-us/azure/devops/marketplace-extensibility`

COMMUNITY FORUMS

Microsoft Azure DevOps Tech Community, `techcommunity.microsoft.com/t5/azure-devops/bd-p/AzureDevOpsForum`

Cloud Native Community, `www.cloudnativecommunity.com/`

Azure Tech Groups, `www.meetup.com/pro/azuretechgroups/`

Azure DevOps on Dev.to, `dev.to/t/azuredevops`

Azure Developer Community, `azdev.reskilll.com`

Microsoft Azure Community, `facebook.com/groups/MicrosoftAzureCommunity`

INDEX

B